Directionally Challenged

Travis Collins has been a good friend to me personally and especially to Woman's Missionary Union. As the pastor of a large church in Richmond, Virginia, Travis recognizes the important role of WMU in the church—leading others to understand, embrace, and live the call of God. Having served as a missionary journeyman, a career missionary in Nigeria, and as a pastor of several different congregations, he speaks from personal experience as a churchman and as one who has lived among the peoples of the world outside the US.

In writing *Live the Call,* I interviewed a number of people about their personal experiences with God's call. Travis was so real about the ups and downs of discovering what it is God desires our lives to be about. But when it came to his call to missions, he said it was as if "God was smiling on my overseas service."

For those who desire to be sensitive to God's call in their lives, one thing is certain: God's call is not a one-time event, nor to a single place of service. God's call is fluid and growing, testing and stretching us as we become mature followers of Christ.

Travis personally acknowledged this reality when he knew God was redirecting him from serving overseas to a US pastorate. With each change in his place of service, Travis said there was a "deep sense of rightness . . . a profound impression in my spirit that my Father and Creator is pleased with this. Living out God's call has its challenges."

As you read this book, you will discover for yourself through the experiences of one who has learned to trust and follow God's call that it is always the right thing to do. We don't have to live our lives confused about which direction to follow. We have a God who stands ready and willing to set us on the right path, a path that leads to joy and fulfillment as well as a purpose that gives meaning to each and every day.

—*Wanda Lee*
Executive Director
Woman's Missionary Union

Directionally Challenged

*How to Find and Follow
God's Course for Your Life*

Travis Collins

NEW HOPE
PUBLISHERS

Birmingham, Alabama

New Hope® Publishers
P. O. Box 12065
Birmingham, AL 35202-2065
www.newhopepublishers.com

Library of Congress Cataloging-in-Publication Data

Collins, Travis.
  Directionally challenged : how to find and follow God's course for your life / Travis Collins.
    p. cm.
  ISBN 978-1-59669-075-2 (sc)
  1. Discernment (Christian theology) 2. Vocation--Christianity. I.
Title.
BV4509.5.C652 2007
248.4--dc22

                            2006039260

ISBN-10: 1-59669-075-5
ISBN-13: 978-1-59669-075-2

N074136 • 0507 • 7M1

Dedicated to my friends at
Woman's Missionary Union
and
Woman's Missionary Union Foundation
—missional-living people
whom I deeply admire

CONTENTS

INTRODUCTION

Keri and I have two sons and a daughter. They are at the ages at which they are asking some of life's defining questions, and I have the privilege of helping them think through those questions. Naturally, I sometimes offer my input even when they don't ask.

Our church is working hard to help people in our church—laypersons, as they are usually called—to discern and embrace their places in the family of God. We have an associate pastor for member mobilization who leads us in that effort. Also, at the time of this writing, I am meeting intermittently with seven college students and two adults in midcareer from our church family who believe they are being drawn to some type of vocational ministry. In addition, people never stop asking questions about the "will of God." Sincere Christ followers long to understand the heart and mind of our Father.

I often speak with people who are in ministerial vocations—pastors and others whose livelihoods come from their ministry. It's not uncommon for people in vocational ministry to struggle with their call, even to the point of wondering if perhaps they should try real estate or insurance or some other line of work.

I have written this book with people like my own sons and daughter in mind, as well as the members of our church family and the vocational ministers I know.

Besides that, I am living my personal call. I'm not living it perfectly. I don't get emails from God. I don't understand fully the ways of the Creator. Never have. Yet I write as one who is attempting, by God's grace, to hear and follow the promptings of the Spirit.

Before we get too far into this, you need to know some of my basic assumptions regarding God's call:

1. We can know, and live out, the purposes for which we were created. Acts 13:36 tells us, "When David had served God's purpose in his own generation, he fell asleep." It is possible for humans like you and me to fulfill God's purposes for us during the fleeting time allotted to us on this earth.

2. God created us with gifts that overlap with His work in the world. No one is called to help meet every need. Yet at the point where the world's needs, God's mission, and our gifts meet—there we find our calling, our purpose for being. And for each of us there are those exciting intersections.

3. Many of us would do a far better job of fulfilling the purposes for which we were created if we were better able to discern those purposes. The age-old question, What is God's will for my life? reflects both our innate longing to do what we were put here by God to do and our difficulty in discerning our God-given roles. One of my prayers for this book is that we will gain some tools that will help us discover God's intentions for our lives.

4. God does communicate with us. Discerning God's call (hearing His voice) is not a simple matter. Yet it is possible to stand at life's many crossroads and know what pleases God. God promised us, "Whether you turn to the right or to the left, your ears will hear a voice behind you saying, 'This is the way; walk in it'" (Isaiah 30:21).

5. Many of us are wandering without a sense of direction, and a COMPASS would be a welcome addition to our journey. Compasses don't answer all the questions of the adventurous traveler. They don't reveal to the traveler, for example, whether to go *around* a mountain or *over* a mountain. Compasses don't reveal every detail of the journey. Compasses do, however, provide direction and inspire confidence for the journey. My primary purpose in writing this book is to help you find and follow your life compass.

6. Call following is not without its challenges. Nothing of any significance comes easily. In the year of this book's publication, my adopted state of Virginia is celebrating the 400th anniversary of the establishment of Jamestown colony. That first English settlement was quite the adventure, but it was not an adventure for the squeamish. I see following God's call as an adventure too and, as in all adventures, hearty constitutions are required.

7. Life's greatest joy comes in actively living out our calls. I am a football official, and I like to observe the dynamics among the players. Picture with me some football players standing on the sideline, watching their teammates out on the field. Why, when a player comes out, does #43 look longingly at the coach, hoping against hope that this time #43 will be the one the coach puts in? Because, though it's fun just being on the team, players on the sideline know the real joy is in the game. Likewise, life's greatest joy is in the arena—in the risky but fulfilling adventure of doing what God had in mind for us when He breathed life into us—not standing on the sideline.

8. Knowing and embracing God's call prevents us from getting sidetracked. The Christian journey is a bit like a walk through a carnival. Remember the hawkers? A young man calls out from the booth where folks are shooting at ducks: "Come and play! Win a great prize!" The gentleman who wants to guess your age and weight declares, "It's just a dollar." Another guy tries to lure men into the tent—"Adults only," he says.

Doesn't your life sometimes seem like that? Invitations abound. There are so many good things to be done, and temptations besides. Getting sidetracked is easy; knowing and embracing God's call empowers us to ignore all those enticements that would sidetrack us. Knowing and embracing God's call keeps us out of those booths and tents of life in which we would squander our resources and go astray.

No one understands this better than the members of Woman's Missionary Union® (WMU®). **My friends at WMU are going to use this book in their annual emphasis, and I cannot miss this opportunity to express my appreciation to them for their single-minded concentration on missions.**

I have said it in a number of venues, and I'm proud to put it in print: WMU is my favorite group of Baptists.

They were marvelous supporters when my wife and I were missionaries to Nigeria. Besides that, they have kept the main thing the main thing since they began in 1888. They could easily have gotten sidetracked in this carnival-like world we live in; yet the people of WMU have been unwaveringly faithful to their call to engage the world through missions and to support missionaries. The members of WMU have demonstrated how a clear discernment of our call, and tenacious commitment to that call, can keep us on track.

If you share the above assumptions, or even if you are willing to consider them, I believe the time we spend together in this book will help you to understand what we often refer to as the will of God. Writing this book has been personally beneficial for me. Sometimes I have had to stop and wrestle with certain things I've written. I'd type and wrestle; wrestle and type. Therefore, I do not offer these words to you frivolously. I offer them to you as convictions— convictions that have made a big difference to me.

So I encourage you to read and wrestle. I pray that reading this book will be as helpful for you as writing it was for me.

YOUR PART IN GOD'S SYMPHONY

I remember singing a song in a youth musical, the title of which was, "Do You Have a Purpose for Life?" I can think of no more profound question.

While you read this, a gentleman will sit in a coffee shop contemplating life. A few days ago he walked out of his office carrying a cardboard box full of family pictures and other items previously found in his mahogany drawers—another casualty of downsizing. Over his cup of coffee he ponders whether the loss of his job is a tragedy, or perhaps an opportunity to find a career that will offer him a genuine sense of purpose. He also wonders whether or not God might have something to say about that.

Tonight a teenager will contemplate suicide. She stands dangerously near the precipice because she has not yet found a satisfactory answer to her question: "Why in the world am I here?"

After she finally got the kids in bed last night, the woman down the street from you sat for a while, rubbing her temples. She is wrestling with a recent invitation to return to the law firm she enjoyed so much before her children were born.

She longs to know what God wants her to do. (Truthfully, she wishes God would just tell her what to do and spare her the agony of deciding.)

Last night a minister of youth had trouble sleeping, for another church has invited him to interview for the open position on their staff. If he were to go to another church, would he be *following* God's call, or *abandoning* it? Or would God be pleased with either choice he makes, as long as his motives are right?

Last Friday a college student left class with a headache. The professor had declared that human beings are coincidental fallout of a cosmic explosion and that there isn't a lot of real meaning to our existence. Up until now that student's only serious interests have been fashions and fraternities, but since Friday she has been wondering if her life truly is a mere accident. The clichés and pat answers she heard growing up in church aren't adequate now. And she longs to know whether, if there is a God, she has a place in His plan.

Next Sunday a missionary will speak in a church somewhere. While he speaks, a high school senior's mind will work overtime: "Being a missionary sounds fascinating....I couldn't do that....I *wouldn't* do that....Missionaries are more spiritual than I am....And the needs are so great....Do they have McDonald's overseas?" Then, at the close of the day, he lies in his bed wondering whether that uneasiness in his heart is a call to be a missionary.

Then there's you and me, of course. In our own ways we, too, wonder about our life's purpose.

Some of us have found that purpose. We are living what our Creator created us to do, and we know it. The waters are not always smooth, but we feel the wind of the Spirit in our sails.

We have found a purpose bigger than ourselves, a cause worth giving our lives to, and something that enables us to make a real difference in the world, and this gives us deep joy.

Others of us are still searching. We want to do things that have meaning, and we want to leave a legacy, but we can't figure out where to start. We'd follow God's plan (at least we *think* we would) if He'd just give us some kind of sign. Without an understanding of where we ought to be headed, we seem to be headed nowhere fast. Yes, some of us—too many of us—are wandering aimlessly.

A college friend of mine loved to quote the late Senator Howell Heflin who intoned in his beautiful Alabama accent: "We ah wanderin' aimlessleh without a gooooal!" My friend must have found those words applicable as he looked around him. I think he was right; a lot of us are wandering aimlessly and goal-lessly. And aimless, goal-less living makes for awfully miserable folks.

So how does one find an aim? A goal? A Christ follower might ask it this way: "How do I find God's will for my life?"

NOT A BLUEPRINT, BUT A MISSION

Unfortunately, I haven't been able to find a lot of Bible verses that deal specifically with God's will for your life. But wait! Please don't close the book! You *can* find direction; you *can* find God's purpose for you. God knows the plans He has for you (Jeremiah 29:11), and you can discover those plans. The truth is, however, that you won't find in Scripture any fail-safe, foolproof, infallible formulas.

I remember being disappointed by that fact when, as a fairly new pastor, I decided to preach my first sermon on finding God's will. I looked in my concordance under *will of God* and expected to find an abundance of passages on the subject. I looked forward to helping members of my flock find God's specific goal for each of them. I was certain I would be able to help them decipher God's blueprint, His individual design, for each of their lives.

Blueprint passages, however, were conspicuously missing.

What I *did* find, and have continued to find, is a lot about God's mission in the world. I have found countless stories about how deeply the Creator is involved in His creation. I have found God's desires for the world, such as:

- His desire that everyone have eternal and abundant life through faith in His Son, Jesus
- His desire that people who are suffering receive care
- His desire that all people be treated fairly
- His desire that those blessed with much would share with those who have little
- His desire that people understand the value of moral boundaries for the living of our lives
- His desire that people embrace His grace—His unconditional, undeserved, unlimited love

I also found in the Scriptures stories of lots of people—rather ordinary folks, most of them—who found their place in God's mission. I didn't ever see where He spelled out His "will for their lives." In fact, I doubt that such a concept ever would have occurred to them (at least not in the self-centered way that we sometimes approach the subject). I did, however, see God direct their paths and prepare them for specific tasks within His plan. Then I saw how they came to sense that God wanted them to do certain things at certain times. I admit, *how* they sensed these things wasn't always very clear.

In other words, the Bible doesn't talk a lot about "God's will for our lives." It *does* talk a lot about how people find great fulfillment and make great contributions by finding their place within God's mission.

Here is another way to look at it. A musician probably won't ask the composer/ conductor, "What is your plan for me?" The musician is more likely to ask, "Is there a part I may play in your symphony?" And that musician's part in the symphony will be determined largely by such things as the instrument the musician has the talent to play, the passion with which she plays, and how well she has developed her gift.

Likewise, a new baseball player is not likely to ask the coach, "Coach, what is your personalized plan for me?" The baseball player is more likely to ask, "Is there a place for me on your team?" And the player's role is going to be determined largely by such things as his particular physical gifts, his devotion to the game, and how well he has honed his God-given skills.

You have a part to play in this symphony, on this team. You have gifts. You have particular passions, talents, and interests. If you will develop your skills, keep your priorities in order, and do your best to obey your Creator, you will find joy and fulfillment in the living of life. You will come to know a deep sense of rightness about the role God chose for you.

That deep sense of rightness about your part in God's mission is your call. Your call, or calling, is that communiqué from God Himself that He is indeed at work in the world, that He wants you to join Him where He is at work, and that *this* is the role God "cut you out for." You don't have to wander aimlessly; you can follow a God-given goal. You can live missionally.

MISSIONAL LIVING

I like the term *missional*; it describes the kind of life that I want to live. *Missional* is not the same as *missions-minded*, although they are not completely unrelated. To be missional simply means to be on a mission—God's mission. A "missional Christ follower" is one who is living *intentionally*—intentionally following God's call.

A missional follower of Jesus has a definite purpose. He or she intentionally and consistently listens for, and obeys, the promptings of God's Spirit. He or she understands God's mission in the world and his or her place in that mission.

Andrea Mullins, in *Intentional Living*, put it like this:

> Intentional living is a lifetime journey of discovery with God. Choosing to live for God's purposes requires a commitment to His mission, or what is called a *missional life*. In other words, intentional living is choosing to commit to God's mission to restore mankind to a relationship with Him.

Missional followers of Jesus are not wandering aimlessly. They intentionally follow a goal, a God-given goal, a goal that originated with the Creator. They see following Jesus as a means of meeting human needs, not as a means of having their own emotional needs met. They know that what they do *matters*. That kind of living, by the way, is not only for people who live on some mystical, higher plane. *You* can be a missional Christ follower.

Leonard Sweet, in *Summoned to Lead,* told of cancer clinics in Europe in which the physician will not attempt treatment before saying, "You must tell me your mission. Why is it that you must live? Specifically, what must you accomplish?" Apparently the physicians believe there is little they can do unless the patient is living with a clear mission.

If an oncologist were to ask you that question, could you answer? Wouldn't it be wonderful to be able to look her in the eye and articulate a clear mission about which you feel passionately? Wouldn't it be even greater if that mission had come from God Himself?

I had lunch not long ago with an old college friend, Greg Powell. Greg is an outstanding financial advisor and has been asked to speak around the country because of his achievement. He told me the key to his success: "I won't talk about people's money until they answer the following questions: What is your mission? What is your passion? What do you really want to do in life? What do you want your legacy to be?"

Greg, like the oncologists, recognizes the importance of a life-mission. The apostle Paul certainly knew *his* life-mission. He began his first letter to Timothy with these words: "Paul, an apostle of Christ Jesus by the command of God our Savior and of Christ Jesus our hope." **How would it feel if you could proclaim your mission and add that you have that mission *by command of God*?** You *can* do that. You can actually obey the royal command of the King of the universe.

GOD STILL SPEAKS, AND WE CAN HEAR HIM

Brownie Hamilton, a member of our congregation, read something in our church's monthly newsletter that really interested her. The Richmond Baptist Association (of which our church is a member) was organizing a mission trip to China. The contact information for the coordinator of the trip, a woman named Ruth, was listed. (Ruth is a member of another church.)

Brownie called Ruth that afternoon, introduced herself, and asked, "How can I get my name on the list for that mission trip to China?" Ruth responded, "May I ask how you got my name?"

Brownie answered, "The Spirit."

Ruth gasped and thought to herself, "Oh my, I've got someone on the phone who thinks the Holy Spirit gave her my name!"

A few minutes into the conversation it was confirmed that Brownie did, indeed, get Ruth's name from "The Spirit." The matter was not quite as mystical as Ruth had imagined, however; "The Spirit" is the name of our church's newsletter.

God doesn't generally speak as clearly as the words printed in the church paper. Yet God does speak. And we can hear Him. I believe that; I've experienced it personally. God never has spoken audibly to me, nor has He sent me a personalized message in print, but I look back at the clear promptings of God's Spirit and am amazed that the Creator of the universe is involved in giving direction to my life. **The certainty of God's call is as ancient as the story of Abraham in Genesis 12 and as recent as the last time you sensed God's clear intentions for**

you. God does still speak. He continues to call those who will listen.

Jesus prayed to the Father, "I have brought you glory on earth by completing the work you gave me to do" (John 17:4). Jesus understood the assignment from His Father. So can we. When God gives us "work to do," that is His "call" for us.

God's call is far too mysterious for us to understand fully. Nevertheless, I believe we all can learn to be better listeners—more able to discern God's initiatives. We can know enough to make good choices. We can know what we need to know when we need to know it. **There are biblical principles that, when embraced, form a conduit for receiving God's signals and a matrix for processing those signals.**

Discernment of God's will is indeed critical, for Warren Wiersbe, in *On Being a Servant,* was right: "God still gives His best to those who let Him write the contract." God inspired the apostle Paul to write, "Do not be foolish, but understand what the Lord's will is" (Ephesians 5:17).

Beyond the concept of *discerning* God's call is the opportunity and responsibility of *following* God's call. While understanding the initiatives of the Father is critical, understanding them is only part of the matter. Even when we get the why, we are left with the how.

It takes courage, conviction, and character to follow God. Just look at the lives of the apostles, or at those folks around you who seem to be following God closely. In this book we will wrestle with both the *discerning of* and the *following of* God's call. I pray that by the time we complete our time together, we both will be living the adventure of following God with new clarity and greater gusto.

That adventure begins with a faith decision—the decision to believe that God still speaks. Once you believe that, from then on it is a matter of learning to listen for God's voice.

CALL DEFINED

I realize the depth into which I am wading, but I must offer a definition of a *call*, so here goes.

> **Call is the ongoing prompting of God's Spirit, confirmed through Scripture, the faith community, intellect, and experience, which communicates: These are your roles in my mission.**

That definition needs an explanation. First, call is ongoing. Call is not a one-time experience at a youth retreat. God's call unfolds throughout our lives.

Second, call is a prompting. Perhaps you are thinking *prompting* is a rather vague term. If so, you would be right. I intentionally use the word *prompting* because our perception of God's activity in our lives is more than a feeling or a thought. I call it a sense, for *sense* implies a broader kind of discernment than that which is possible through mere emotion or intellect. I believe we *sense* God's call. By that I mean we experience a supernatural, spiritual impression that God is communicating with us. Paul wrote that "the Spirit himself testifies with our spirit that we are God's children" (Romans 8:16). Likewise, it is this supernatural communication of the Holy Spirit with our spirits that enables us to be, as Scripture says both of Jesus and His followers, "led by the Spirit." Of course to be "led by the Spirit" is to be "called."

Third, these mysterious promptings are confirmed through the Scriptures, input from fellow believers, intellect, and experience. Affirmations of our sense of God's leadership provide the clarity and confidence necessary to follow God's call.

Fourth, God's call is to *roles*, not merely to a *role*. God's will for us is not limited to geography or vocation. It includes His intentions regarding such elements of our lives as our families, our lifestyles, our priorities, and our specific actions in particular situations.

Finally, God's purposes for us always fit within His "Big Picture." He leads us to our roles in *His* mission, rather than unveiling some sort of script for the world with you or me as the lead character. God is the star of this drama; not us.

FOUR LEVELS OF CALL

There are actually four levels, or kinds, of call.

1. The call into a relationship with God through Jesus

"As Jesus was walking beside the Sea of Galilee, he saw two brothers, Simon called Peter and his brother Andrew. They were casting a net into the lake, for they were fishermen. 'Come, follow me,' Jesus said, 'and I will make you fishers of men.' At once they left their nets and followed him. Going on from there, he saw two other brothers, James son of Zebedee and his brother John. They were in a boat with their father Zebedee, preparing their nets. Jesus called them, and

immediately they left the boat and their father and followed him" (Matthew 4:18–22).

"The Spirit and the bride say, 'Come!' And let him who hears say, 'Come!' Whoever is thirsty, let him come; and whoever wishes, let him take the free gift of the water of life" (Revelation 22:17).

The first call you hear is God's call into relationship with Him through faith in Jesus.

I spent two years (1981–83) alongside career missionaries as a missionary journeyman in Venezuela. There I worked at a boys' home in a town called Mene Grande, and in that home for boys I met a Guajira Indian boy named José Gregorio. His mom apparently was not sure who José's father was; and because she was either unable or unwilling to care for the boy, she had taken him to live with an elderly Venezuelan couple. When the boy became old enough to go to school, this elderly couple felt they couldn't rear him properly and began to look for someone who could provide for him.

If there ever was a "lost sheep," it was José. No real family. No real place in Venezuelan society. And that little Guajira Indian boy with the bronze skin and piercing black eyes came to live at the boys' home where I worked.

We came to have a close relationship. One day we were in my matchbox-sized office talking about what it means to follow Jesus. José had been exposed in various times and places to what following Jesus means, but we were reviewing those spiritual truths. In the middle of our conversation he interrupted me and said, *"Hermano Travis, mi corazón está haciendó poom poom poom poom poom."* (Brother

Travis, my heart is going poom poom poom poom poom.)
I asked "What do you think that is, José?" And he answered,
"Creo que es Jesus" (I believe it's Jesus).

Maybe you have been feeling a stirring within you lately,
and you know as well as José did that the Spirit of Jesus is
making a claim on your life. Many of you responded to that
call of God's Spirit some time ago. If you have not made a
decision to follow Jesus, then I encourage you to make that
fundamental decision. God does call, and His basic call is
that we follow Jesus and thus receive life at its best and life
that never ends.

2. The call to a way of life, including lifestyle and vocation

> *"Listen to me, you islands; hear this, you distant
> nations: Before I was born the LORD called me; from my
> birth he has made mention of my name" (Isaiah 49:1).*

> *"Paul, called to be an apostle of Christ Jesus by the
> will of God" (1 Corinthians 1:1).*

Besides a commitment to Jesus that changes our eternal
destinies, God calls us to a way of life—a kind of living that
reflects the character and mission of God. It changes our
lifestyle. God's purposes for us include fundamental elements of our lives such as our moral choices, how we spend
our money, how we spend our leisure time, the causes in
which we invest ourselves, and our values. God's call is a
call to a godly lifestyle.

God's call can also lead to a change of vocation. Keith
Ferrazzi wrote in *Never Eat Alone:*

People get overwhelmed by the decisions they have to make about their jobs....There are too many choices, it seems. We end up shifting our focus to talents we don't have and careers that don't quite fit. Many of us respond by simply falling into whatever comes down the pike without ever asking ourselves some very important questions.

The first of those very important questions is what God is calling us to do. God's call certainly extends to how we will spend the workweek.

A young Christ follower, just finishing the university or some technical training, prays, "God, help me to find the right field of work, and the right place to work."

A person in midcareer prays, "God, I have this unsettled kind of feeling, like perhaps You are wanting to lead me into a new vocation. Are you changing my direction? Opening a new door?"

A new retiree prays, "Lord, You have given me wonderful opportunities and I have acquired certain skills. How, now that my schedule is more flexible, may I serve You with what I have?"

A stay-at-home parent prays, "Lord, I always have felt this is what you are pleased to see me doing. Is this indeed what you want for me?"

A high school senior with academic gifts prays, "Well, God, I guess my job for the foreseeable future is to further my education. Please help me to make a good choice regarding the school where I will study. Oh, and, if You're not too busy, some clue about a major course of study sure would be nice!"

All these folks are appropriately attempting to tune in to God's vocational call.

A noteworthy factor here is that most who read this book have vocational opportunities that some others don't have. People in many societies have limited employment options. Even in our country it is a lot easier for some than it is for others to choose how they will earn a living. Nevertheless, all of us can know God's pleasure in our vocations. When a person's employment opportunities are limited, then that person simply has to find God's purposes in the employment in which the person currently serves. Those of us who have a wide range of employment options have a considerable responsibility to seek God's leadership and make good vocational decisions.

3. Call to specific acts

"From the east I summon a bird of prey; from a far-off land, a man to fulfill my purpose" (Isaiah 46:11).

"I, even I, have spoken; yes, I have called him. I will bring him, and he will succeed in his mission" (Isaiah 48:15). (This refers to God choosing Cyrus as king of Persia in order to defeat the Babylonians and free the Israelites from their Babylonian exile. That was God's call to Cyrus for a specific act.)

Paul planned to go to Bithynia, *"but the Spirit of Jesus would not allow them to"* (Acts 16:7). So they went ahead to Macedonia, *"concluding that God had called us to preach the gospel to them"* (Acts 16:10). He also told the good folks at Ephesus, *"I will come back if it is God's will"* (Acts 18:21). And he declared later, *"Compelled by the Spirit, I am going to Jerusalem"* (Acts 20:22).

Jennifer sits down in the company cafeteria with a plate of steamed vegetables, her low-fat candy bar, and a diet soda. As she sits down, a young woman from two cubicles down takes the seat across from her. Jennifer's slim co-worker has a cheeseburger, fries, a milkshake to wash it down, and a doughnut for dessert. Jennifer quickly calculates her co-worker's calories and moans at the injustices of life.

Soon the young woman is pouring out her heart to Jennifer: she just found out she is pregnant, and that is not good news. She is scared, and contemplating an abortion.

There is an instant connection between the two. Jennifer finds herself offering insights that appear genuinely helpful to her frightened young co-worker. Jennifer is able to comfort her, and they agree to meet for lunch the next day.

On her way back upstairs, Jennifer is troubled by her co-worker's crisis. Yet she feels a deep satisfaction about having had that conversation. Talking to that young woman really felt good to Jennifer. Then Jennifer remembers the words of the woman who spoke at church on the previous Sunday about the crisis pregnancy center. While she listened to the director of that center make her plea for volunteers, Jennifer had felt the same stirring she felt in the cafeteria listening to the young woman pour out her heart.

By the time she closes her eyes that night she has spoken with the crisis pregnancy center's director, and by the weekend Jennifer knows it: she has been called by God to volunteer at the crisis pregnancy center. Years down the road, after having spent almost every Saturday morning as a volunteer at the center, she will look back with gratitude on that week, when God used a frightened young woman and a crisis pregnancy center director to *call* her. Jennifer has found one of her primary roles in God's mission.

Of course God's call is not always so dramatic. God might call you, for example, to speak a particular word to your neighbor. You both have taken the trash can to the road at the same time and you meet there in the street. After exchanging comments about the weather, you sense something going on in your spirit. Your heart races a bit. You believe God wants you to say something. Believing God's Spirit is indeed behind this, you blurt out, "Is there anything I can pray about for you?" Your neighbor, who usually is not open to spiritual discussions, gets an inquisitive look on his face. "Funny you should ask," he says. "I could use some prayers for my family." You have responded to God's call.

Whether it is to volunteer for a ministry or speak to a neighbor, God calls us to specific acts.

4. Corporate call

While the fairly new Christians in Antioch were worshipping and fasting, *"the Holy Spirit said, 'Set apart for me Barnabas and Saul for the work to which I have called them'"* (Acts 13:2).

No group can do everything, so a faithful family of believers will seek God's unique plan for them. When a particular church (or any Christian organization for that matter) gets as serious about their role as did the Christians in Antioch, they will be able to sense God's desires for their community of faith. Together they can recognize what God has for that specific body of Christ followers.

IN THIS BOOK . . .

What I do in this book will apply primarily to the **call to a way of life** and the **call to specific acts**. Of course if any reader has not settled the first call—the **call to follow Jesus**—then you need to back up and consider that one seriously. It is a fundamental step toward understanding what you were created for. Besides that, your eternal life hinges on that basic decision.

I won't address directly the fourth kind of call, the **corporate call**. Yet I assume that if we and the fellow members of our faith communities are discerning and living our *personal* calls, that will make understanding and following our *corporate* call much easier. Furthermore, the principles regarding a personal, individual call are germane when applied to a group.

A great passion of my life is football officiating. As a referee, I find it fascinating to watch football teams and their quarterbacks. The next time you get a chance, watch how, in the huddle and just before every play, everyone on the team listens for the voice of the quarterback. Not that of the cheerleaders. Not that of the critics. One voice. They want to hear the plan in the huddle, and on the line they want to hear the signal to move. Likewise, God's call, when we listen for it and hear it, gives us a laser-like focus and clear direction in the midst of a cacophony of the world's voices. God's call tells us what, how, and when. In the next chapter we will consider how we can listen intently to the voice of God Himself.

HEARING GOD'S VOICE

2

I guess some folks will question whether or not humans actually can recognize the voice of God. I believe we can. Jesus seems to have agreed, for He declared, "The sheep listen to his voice. He calls his own sheep by name and leads them out....His sheep follow him because they know his voice" (John 10:3–4).

It isn't easy, at least for me, to discern the voice of God's Spirit. Charles Poole, in *Don't Cry Past Tuesday,* says it's like driving down the interstate when you're looking for a station on the car radio. You come upon your favorite song, but the reception is bad and the sound is faint. It's hard to hear the music through the static and it's fading in and out. Yet you continue to listen, though you have to strain, because the song is so meaningful to you.

God's voice is a bit like the song on that distant radio station. We have to strain to hear. But His sheep listen for, and recognize, His voice.

When you and I see a flock of sheep, we don't see individual sheep; we just see *sheep.* A sea of sheep. Not so with the shepherd. He sees *sheep*—individual sheep. He sees Mutton Head over there, and he remembers when Mutton Head spent half a wintry night in the thorns before the shepherd found him. And the shepherd sees Curly over there; he knows Curly's story too. And there is Wooley. And there is Lamb Chop. The shepherd knows them all. Knows their names. Knows their stories.

Likewise, when most of us see people we just see *people*, not persons. But not so with Jesus. He knows us. He knows you. Has numbered the hairs on your head. Knows your dreams. Knows your hurts. Calls you by name. **One who knows us that personally knows how to get through to us.** We sheep can identify His voice.

WHAT AM I LISTENING FOR?

How do I perk up my ears? And how do I know when I've heard it? Let's imagine something: Your doctor says that you need a new hobby to balance out your life and minimize your stress. He suggests bird watching. Thus you join an expedition into the forest to find the elusive blue-breasted caterwauler. Once in an area where it is believed blue-breasted caterwaulers nest, everyone falls silent and the guide speaks. "I am going to position you people in strategic locations 50 yards apart. Your assignment is to listen for the call of the blue-breasted caterwauler. These bashful birds move stealthily among the leaves, so you are not likely to see them. Therefore, you must listen carefully for their songs."

You're thinking, "How am I supposed to know what a blue-breasted caterwauler sounds like?" At that moment the guide reaches into his backpack and pulls out a small CD player. He plays a recording of the beautiful and distinct call of the bird in question. He plays it several times, enough for even you to believe that if you hear it, you will recognize it.

An hour later, you are in your secluded spot and about to drift off to sleep. You hear something. It sounds like... no, it couldn't be. But the song continues. And, yes, it *is* the blue-breasted caterwauler! It is the same song that you heard played by the guide! The bird's call is as beautiful as it is inimitable. You wouldn't have recognized it, though, if you hadn't known what you were listening for.

So, when we talk about hearing a call from God, what exactly are you listening for? And how do you know if it is truly God you are hearing?

You are listening for a deep sense of rightness. God's voice comes as a profound impression that we are being directed toward a decision. Deep in our spirits there comes an "ought-ness" if God is guiding our steps.

I was six months out of college and living in Venezuela. I believe I could take you to the spot in Caracas where, walking across the street after a church youth rally, I experienced a deep sense of rightness, an "ought-ness," about being a career missionary. Within a few yards I went from not even thinking about the future to a decision that I would enroll in seminary after my two-year assignment, and go overseas as an international missionary. There was nothing all that dramatic; it just hit me—this is *right;* it is *who I am;* it is *what God had in mind for me all along.*

For me, God's voice sounds like a quiet, confident, unwavering yes in my gut. "Gut feelings," of course, need confirmation.

Dan McBride sang, "This must be the will of the Lord

because it seems so right to me." Is that how we determine the will of the Lord? A feeling? Well, just a few sentences ago I suggested that God communicates His will for us through a deep sense of rightness. So how can we confirm that this nebulous deep sense of rightness is actually the voice of God?

Have you ever read a story from the Bible and wondered how the people in the story knew with such clarity what God was saying? How did Paul know for certain that God's Spirit was preventing him from going into the province of Asia (Acts 16:6)? How did Abraham know that God was calling him to leave his country on a pilgrimage to an uncertain destination (Genesis 12:1)? And how can we know it when God is calling us? What signs should we look for? Is there a checklist? How can we confirm that our gut feeling is God's prompting?

Hearing and confirming the voice of God is not without its mystery. In fact, I saw something one day that troubled me. It was an advertisement for a book on finding the will of God. That ad read, "Now, knowing and doing the will of God does not have to be a mystery anymore."

I disagree. I think that for sinful, finite humans to know and do the will of the holy, infinite Creator and Master of the universe, there always will be a certain element of uncertainty. No preacher or product can truly take the mystery out of God's will.

Yet we don't have to be paralyzed by that mystery and uncertainty. I believe we can know enough to make the right choices. We can know what we need to know when we need to know it. We can become so in tune with God's Spirit that we hear His voice. Then we can find affirmation and confirmation that we have indeed received a message from heaven. That affirmation and confirmation will be the focus of the next few chapters.

I will present to you a COMPASS—a tool for helping to verify the inaudible voice of God—just a bit farther into the book. Of course, there is no secret key, no foolproof methodology, for knowing the will of God. There are, however, some essentials, some prerequisites, for discerning the Shepherd's voice. Here are a few.

A PERSONAL, GROWING, REAL RELATIONSHIP WITH GOD

Henry Blackaby, in *Experiencing God,* stated: "The key to knowing God's voice is not a formula. It is not a method we can follow. Rather, knowing God's voice comes from an intimate love relationship with God." If my children face a tough decision tomorrow, and if they want to do what I would want them to do, they probably will know in their hearts what I would say. They might call and ask, but more than likely they will know what I am going to tell them. For they know me; they spend time with me, talking with me. Likewise, if you want to know God's plan for you, then cultivate your relationship with Him.

In cultivating my own relationship with God, I have found fasting to be a particularly meaningful practice. **Because not much is said about fasting nowadays, let's look closely at this important spiritual discipline.**

I'm certain that fasting seems odd to many. That's understandable, for the idea of fasting hasn't been talked about much for a long time. But those who lived in the days of the Bible probably would be surprised that fasting seems so strange to us.

In Matthew 6:16, for example, we read the words of Jesus: *"When you fast, do not look somber as the hypocrites do."* Note that Jesus said, *"When* you fast," apparently assuming that fasting would be one of His disciples' spiritual disciplines.

Fasting simply means going for a determined period of time without food for the sake of enhancing our communion with God. In the Bible, fasting is always accompanied by prayer.

There are no rules when it comes to fasting. This is a decision you make, as best you understand God's intentions for you. One possibility is a 24-hour fast. A person could eat breakfast, for example, and then not eat anything until the next morning. Or one might have dinner, and then not eat again until breakfast of the second morning. Some might choose a weeklong fast, during which one might, for instance, skip lunches for an entire week and spend those lunch hours in prayer.

During the fast you could drink water (and/or maybe a sports drink or fruit juices). Of course you should be physically able before you fast; don't jeopardize your health. For most of us, however, fasting is completely healthy.

Fasting is certainly appropriate whenever we are facing big decisions or big issues (as in Ezra 8:21–23). When we need to hear a word from the Lord, fasting makes us uncommonly attentive. Acts 13:2 says that while they were worshipping and fasting, the Holy Spirit spoke! Anytime you sense a need for an intense relationship with God, fasting can help facilitate that.

There is nothing magical about fasting. And this is certainly not a means of manipulating God, for He cannot be manipulated. However, fasting does demonstrate to God how serious we are about our reliance on Him. And the simple act of going without a meal or meals intensifies our connection with our heavenly Father.

God honors our attempts to relate to Him with our whole hearts. He even invites us to demonstrate our wholehearted commitment by fasting. *"Even now,"* says the Lord, *"return to me with all your heart, with fasting"* (Joel 2:12). I believe fasting gets our hearts in tune to hear God's call more clearly. I have found fasting to be an enriching experience in my own life; my communion with God is simply more intense on those occasional days when I fast than on other days.

Through fasting and other spiritual disciplines we deepen our relationship with our Father/Creator. Please understand, however, that the aim of cultivating a relationship with God is not to obtain a blueprint for our lives. A relationship with God is not a means to an end. The relationship *itself* is the end, the goal. Knowing God's will is a consequence, a result—not the *goal*—of knowing God.

OPEN HEARTS

In Acts 16:14, the Bible says of Lydia: "The Lord opened her heart to respond to Paul's message." What was it like, I wonder, for God to open Lydia's heart? Did she unexpectedly find herself interested in what this traveling preacher had to say? Did Paul's message that had seemed so implausible suddenly seem arrestingly true?

The quest to hear from God requires our prayers that God will give us open, sensitive hearts—hearts like Lydias and like that of José Gregorio in the story I told in the last chapter—hearts that recognize when they go *poom poom poom* if it is the work of God's Spirit.

OPEN EYES

Norman Burnes said that when he was a missionary in Greece he often would take the 30-minute bus ride from their home into the center of Athens. Norman is a refreshingly chivalrous man, so naturally, when there were no seats left and a woman boarded the bus, Norman would stand and give her his seat. One day a stranger shared with Norman a trick for not having to give up his seat. "Just pretend you are asleep," the fellow traveler advised, "and when you get to your stop you get off!"

"Close your eyes and ignore other folks," the man implied, "and you won't have to feel badly about not letting them sit down."

I fear too many of us go through life with our eyes closed so that the hurts around us won't make us feel bad. We tend to avoid messy situations, steer away from the depressed areas of the city, and close our eyes to vulnerable people all around us. We don't want to get involved; life is just easier that way. But it also prevents our seeing where God is at work.

Jesus came, He told us, not for the well but for the sick, not for the found but for the lost. If we spend all our time among the well and the found, and close our eyes to the sick and the lost, we have little chance of discerning where God wants us to invest our lives. A sincere desire to see what God wants us to do with our lives will result in a willingness not to ignore people's needs. If we want to know God well enough to respond to His voice, we have to identify with people with whom He identifies, and those who are hurting are precious to God. Remember the words of Jesus in Matthew 25:40: *"I tell you the truth, whatever you did for one of the least of these brothers of mine, you did for me."*

I don't know of anyone who has discerned the will of God while closing their eyes to people around them who are in need.

OPEN BIBLES

I never hear God speak as clearly as I would like, but I believe He speaks. Often God speaks to us through Scripture.

Our daughter, Brennan, was sad when we first told her that a move to Richmond was likely. (At the time she was a 14-year-old with a boyfriend.) Then, two mornings later, she announced, "Last night I was reading in my quiet time the story of Job—how God told him to leave his people and his country and go to a new place."

"Might that have been Abraham?" I asked.

"Whoever," Brennan said.

Then she told Keri and me, "I thought maybe that story was a sign that we should go to Virginia."

Now *that's* cool. God does speak through His Word. I have never seen a passage that begins, "Travis, this is what you are to do." Yet God speaks through the examples and principles of Scripture.

SURRENDERED WILLS

"Therefore, I urge you, brothers, in view of God's mercy, to offer your bodies as living sacrifices, holy and pleasing to God—this is your spiritual act of worship" (Romans 12:1). God is interested in more important things than our self-image. God is interested in people living rightly and treating others fairly. God is interested in seeing hurting people be comforted, and in seeing lost people come to Jesus. God is far more interested in those things than in our fickle self-images. You and I are not the center of the universe; God is. So we must surrender our agendas to His agenda. A willingness to surrender our wills to His is a prerequisite for hearing the voice of the Good Shepherd.

One of my favorite memories from my days as a missionary in Nigeria is about the *Babalawo*—the "father of mysteries" —the "medicine man" who practiced *juju,* or black magic. A Nigerian pastor and I, together with a couple of young adults from the church, spoke candidly with this Babalawo one Sunday afternoon in his mud house. We explained that black magic is of Satan and does not please God. We spoke of Jesus as the Lord and King and as greater than all other powers. This was not the first time the Babalawo had heard this; the Christians in the village had been praying for him and speaking to him of Jesus. He had been attending worship services at the church, and God's Spirit had been working in his heart.

That Sunday afternoon, after we had talked for a while, the man expressed his desire to follow Jesus completely. Thrilled that we had been honored to reap the harvest for which so many had worked, we prayed with him.

Following the prayer, the Babalawo instructed us to gather all his juju into a big bag. He was seated on the floor and he began to direct us, pointing to all those things that he wanted us to take—the gourds (calabashes) and sacks that contained various powders and potions used for such things as charms and curses and incantations. We finally gathered everything, all his juju, in a big bag. "You can do whatever you want with those things," he said. "Burn them, throw them away, whatever you wish."

After we prayed a prayer of thanksgiving, we prepared to leave. But before we could get out the door the old man stopped us, and he began to sing a song that he had heard at church. It was one of the most surreal experiences I can remember. He was singing in Yoruba the hymn he'd often heard the Christians sing at church: "I Surrender All." He had just placed his livelihood and social status in a gunny sack. It was quite an unusual and moving experience. In many ways he had just placed his life in a bag; he had offered it all as his gift to God. That is what it meant for an old Babalawo in Nigeria to follow Jesus.

That also is what it means for you and me to follow Jesus. A call to follow Jesus and to fulfill the Father's desire for us is a call to self-sacrifice, a call to offer all that we have and are to God. **It is a call to renounce the selfishness that comes so naturally to us and that gets such reinforcement by our culture.** This is what Paul was saying in his letter to the Romans, *"Take your everyday, ordinary life—your sleeping, eating, going-to-work, and walking-around life—and place it before God as an offering"* (Romans 12:1 *The Message*).

Careful, now! Don't equate surrender with misery. To

follow God's call does not require our sacrifice of a wonderful life. In losing our life, we find it (Matthew 10:39). Read on!

A RECOGNITION OF OUR
PASSIONS AND GIFTS

"For we are God's workmanship, created in Christ Jesus to do good works, which God prepared in advance for us to do" (Ephesians 2:10).

"Before I formed you in the womb I knew you; before you were born I set you apart" (Jeremiah 1:5).

"There are different kinds of gifts...different kinds of service...different kinds of working, but the same God works all of them in all men" (1 Corinthians 12:4, 5, 6).

God is wise beyond measure. When He wove you together in your mother's womb, He conferred upon you certain passions and gifts as preparation for His call. This matter of passions and gifts is crucial evidence of God's call—so crucial that we will explore them in more detail in the next chapter when I present the idea of a COMPASS.

As a teenager, I sat with other staffers on a balcony at a Christian camp one night chatting with a missionary. He longed for us to understand that a decision to be a missionary wouldn't rule out any further possibility of enjoying life. "When you believe you have found the young woman God wants you to marry," he suggested, as an example, "she will be attractive to you. She will be engaging, appealing, and someone you will want to share your life with. God is not going to lead you to someone you'd be miserable with.

"In the same way," he continued, "when God leads you to a vocation, He doesn't want to make you unhappy. He will lead you to that which you find exciting, engaging, and fulfilling." That missionary changed the way I look at God's leadership, whether it be for a vocation or less momentous decisions. I came to understand that following a divine call is joyous, not tortuous.

But hold on a second! Stop right there!

Before we go on I have to offer a caveat: Don't you go thinking that God's first priority is to make you happy. I sure don't intend to give you that impression. On occasion, joining God in His mission to the world requires our willingness to do something we don't particularly enjoy and for which we are not particularly gifted. In the Big Picture, yes, God calls us for what He has gifted us. Let's not ignore our responsibility to step out of our comfort zones from time to time, however, to be the hands of Jesus in the world.

A lot of folks who can barely swing a hammer have made great contributions by helping build houses through Habitat for Humanity. Others who don't particularly enjoy nursing homes set aside their repulsions and minister there regularly. Many who are shy by nature swallow hard and engage their neighbors in conversations about spiritual issues. Our roles in God's mission sometimes stretch us.

Now that we've got that settled, let's move on.

We can have that deep sense of rightness that comes when God speaks. There is indeed something mystical about that, and discerning His voice is not easy. Yet I believe God does communicate with us so that we can hear Him.

Larnelle Harris sings, "When God calls...we tremble at His bidding with our feet on holy ground." It is indeed a sobering, awesome thing when the Maker of the universe calls. I believe you can know it when He does. In the next chapter we will look at some criteria by which to gauge our "hunches" about God's call.

THE COMPASS 3

There is no more essential navigational tool than the compass. If rule number one of travel is "Go in the right direction," then knowing which direction is right is no small matter.

I can just see it in the eyes of some of the readers: Your personality is just not going to let you be content with general principles, is it? You realize there is inevitable mystery in seeking God's will, but you still want a formula. You want something to check off, a questionnaire to complete, or an instrument to consult. You're not looking for a crystal ball, but a map would be nice. Well, maybe I can help. But first…

Might God want you to struggle? I must warn you that God might just want you to struggle a little bit. J. Oswald Sanders, the great missions leader, wrote in *Spiritual Leadership:*

> We naively think that the more we grow as Christians, the easier it will be to discern the will of God. But the opposite is often the case. God treats the mature leader as a mature adult, leaving more and more to his or her spiritual

discernment and giving fewer bits of tangible guidance than in earlier years....Hudson Taylor [once] said how in his younger days things came so clearly, so quickly to him. "But," he said, "now as I have gone on, and God has used me more and more, I seem often to be like a man going along in a fog. I do not know what to do." But when the time came to act, God always responded to His servant's trust.

Moreover, Brennan Manning, in *Ruthless Trust,* told the story of James Kavanaugh, who went to work for three months with Mother Teresa in Calcutta. Kavanaugh was trying to figure out how to spend the rest of his life. In his first conversation with Mother Teresa she asked him, "What can I do for you?" "I want you to pray for me," he answered.

"What do you want me to pray for," she asked. And he voiced his deep desire—that which had brought him all the way from the US: "Pray that I have clarity."

Mother Teresa was firm: "No, I will not do that." He asked why not, and she answered, "Clarity is the last thing you are clinging to and must let go of." "But you always seem to have clarity," he told her. She laughed. **"I have never had clarity; what I have always had is trust. So I will pray that you trust God."**

So don't get your hopes up; the kind of clarity you seek might not be forthcoming. Nevertheless, in this chapter we will try to find some specific means of confirming that we are hearing God's voice. I cannot promise definitive signs; but indications are possible. There are corroborations we can consider—clues, if you will—in the attempt to hear from God.

A COMPASS

I want to suggest for you a COMPASS, a life COMPASS. In this book, it's the closest thing to a formula you're going to get.

A compass is a device used to determine geographical direction. This helpful instrument usually has a magnetic needle (or needles) designed to align with the earth's magnetic field. The needle points north and the user gets his or her bearings based on that.

Anyone willing to launch out into the unknown needs a compass. A compass is not a mere novelty; it is an indispensable navigational tool used by travelers for finding directions. The best I can tell, compasses were first used by daring mariners in the 1300s. A compass is the tool of adventurers, not couch potatoes.

The compass cannot provide details of the journey ahead. It is not like the newfangled global positioning system in some of your cars; it does not tell you every turn to take even before you reach the turn. A compass also does not remove difficulties or resolve dilemmas. It does not settle disagreements among the explorers as to which should be the next step in the expedition. It does point the way, however, and without a "way pointer" the traveler is in trouble.

The elements that you will find in this COMPASS offer strong indications that God is indeed calling you to something. These are trusted indicators that Christians can use to discern God's particular callings in their lives. Usually one of them alone is not enough to give a person confirmation. But when several of these indicators begin pointing in the same direction, you may have a calling to consider. These indicators form the acronym COMPASS: constancy, observation by others, motive, peculiar passions, aptitudes, seasoning, and sensible decision making.

Warning: These indicators I have chosen do not replace the basic guides of the Christian life— the lordship of Christ, the revelation given us in the Bible, and the Christian's communion with God in prayer. These will always be your first directional guides. If you feel you are being led in a direction that is contrary to the witness of Scripture or the example of Jesus Christ, absolutely mistrust that direction. Throw it out. It is not from God. But if you have a consistent interest, affirmed by other Christians, and an aptitude in an area that is in line with God's mission in the world and consistent with the Spirit of Jesus, you should probably start exploring whether this is a calling for you.

While these COMPASS indicators will not offer you a blueprint, they can help you find the right direction. When accompanied by spiritual disciplines, and a heart that is sensitive to the promptings of God's Spirit, consideration of these factors should be helpful as you, a finite human, seek to understand the mind of infinite God. Considering my compass has been helpful to me.

Let's begin to explore the seven areas of the COMPASS. These are directional indicators that may help you find your calling.

COMPASS

Constancy • •Peculiar passions

Observation by others • • Aptitudes

Motive • • Seasoning

• Sensible decision making

C—Constancy

Is there something you just can't shake? A vision that won't go away? A constant concern for a certain need and a consistent desire to meet that need? Then you might be the recipient of a divine call.

Not so long ago I met with a group of women who soon will open a home for teenage girls. It is a marvelous story of how a woman named Gwen Siler had a vision that wouldn't go away—a vision for a Christian ministry to young women with eating disorders. Despite a steady stream of setbacks Gwen kept following the dream that wouldn't die.

There was a 49-acre piece of property, for example, that Gwen believed God wanted her to have. More than one "sign" had confirmed for Gwen that it was on this piece of God's earth that the vision for the ministry should be implemented. The property, however, was just too expensive at first. Then she had the opportunity to buy it, but it slipped through her hands. Twice. The first time she couldn't close due to a lack of financing and the second time because someone else bought the property. At several junctures it looked to many of us like her vision was just going to disappear into the fog. She even began to appear a bit quixotic to some. But Gwen kept plodding. Kept praying. Kept expecting.

All the while, Rebecca Jones had an undying passion for young women with unplanned pregnancies. For years Rebecca had been drawing up plans for some type of ministry to young women in trouble. Both Gwen and Rebecca are in our church, and when they found out about their similar passions, the confluence of their visions seemed blessed by God.

As I write this, Gwen, Rebecca, and their ministry partners are about to open Northfield, a Christ-centered, residential ministry staffed by an impressive group of compassionate professionals. They will provide referral, analysis, treatment, and follow-up for young women with eating disorders or unplanned pregnancies. Would you like to guess where it is going to be located? Yep, in the plantation-style home on that very piece of property in Cumberland County, Virginia, that once appeared to some to be a pipe dream. It is absolutely one of the most inspiring stories of faith and perseverance that I've ever known.

One day I commented on how unrelenting Gwen had been. "I can't help it," she said. "I can't lay the burden down. This dream keeps haunting and driving and prodding me." Establishing this Christ-centered ministry to young women has been Gwen's call, and now is Rebecca's call, and the call of others who have gotten on board. (That's another thing about a call—it's often infectious.)

If you catch a vision for a particular ministry, but your interests soon shift to something else, then your good idea was probably no more than that—a good idea. We often are intrigued by ministry opportunities, but we cannot meet every need or right every wrong. One of the signs of a God-given call is constancy—a tug that won't go away toward a need that you can meet.

Do you remember God's call to Samuel? Samuel was lying in the quiet darkness when God's voice disturbed Samuel's rest. It was on the fourth time, and after Eli's counsel, that Samuel finally figured out it was God calling. After that fourth call, Samuel answered, *"Speak, for your servant is listening"* (1 Samuel 3:10).

Do you remember God's call to Jeremiah? That prophet described his intense sense of purpose in these words: *"His word is in my heart like a fire, a fire shut up in my bones. I am weary of holding it in; indeed, I cannot"* (Jeremiah 20:9).

The missionary Paul wrote, "I am compelled to preach. Woe to me if I do not preach the gospel!" (1 Corinthians 9:16). Paul was an apostle simply because he couldn't do otherwise.

Do you have a recurring, compelling vision—something that just won't let you go? That might just be your divine call. As with Samuel, when you lie in your bed at night do you have a persistent sense that you ought to be doing something specific with your life? Perhaps it is God trying to get your attention. As with Jeremiah, is there a fire in your bones? It might be God who placed that flame in your frame. As with Paul, do you feel absolutely *compelled* to do something? Perhaps God is the compeller.

O—Observation by Others

I never will make a big decision without the full support of my most trusted adviser, my wife, Keri. She is wiser than I am. She thinks things through better than I do. And she is more spiritual than I am. And you'd better believe I ask for her observations when I'm making a decision. (Of course, if the decision affects both of us, we make it together.)

God also has faithfully brought others into my life to help me discern His call.

It was one of the most pivotal moments in my life. I had come down the stairs from the cafeteria in Samford University's student center. At the bottom of the stairs a professor stopped me. "Are you Travis Collins?" If you had known me when I was in college, you would know that it was not necessarily a good thing for a professor to be looking for me. With some trepidation I admitted that I answer to that name.

The professor introduced himself as Bill Cowley. He barely knew who I was, but he was sensitive enough to God's Spirit, and observant enough of people, to discern that down inside of me was a latent call to international missions. For two years he took me to lunch, invited me to his home, mentored and challenged me, pulled no punches with me, and gently nudged me toward the two-year Missionary Journeyman Program. The Missionary Journeyman Program set the course for my life. It was nothing less than an act of God that Dr. Cowley introduced himself to me at the bottom of that staircase. His observation of me—of something I didn't see in myself—set me on my God-planned course.

When I imagine the relationship between Paul and Timothy, I think it must have been a bit like that between Bill Cowley and myself. Paul wrote to Timothy, *"I have been reminded of your sincere faith, which first lived in your grandmother Lois and in your mother Eunice and, I am persuaded, now lives in you also. For this reason I remind you to fan into flame the gift of God"* (2 Timothy 1:5–6). In those words Paul's affection for his young protégé is obvious. Yet Paul did not hesitate to be frank when Timothy needed it.

Paul began his first letter to Timothy with an interesting mandate: "As I urged you when I went into Macedonia, stay there in Ephesus." Timothy was young and perhaps easily disheartened. And there certainly were plenty of potentially disheartening things about the church in Ephesus. Perhaps Timothy had expressed openly to Paul his desire to leave— to go to an easier assignment—to move to greener pastures. But Paul held Timothy's feet to the fire: "Timothy, you stay in Ephesus."

In Paul's relationship with Timothy, I see what you and I need from those whose observations will help us discern God's call: genuine concern for Timothy's well-being, words of encouragement, a readiness to address the chinks in Timothy's armor when warranted, and the wisdom to give sound counsel.

You need to look for your personal Pauls and Bill Cowleys. God has them for you—people who love you and who are kind enough, honest enough, candid enough, and wise enough to give you good counsel. **Maybe you need to initiate a conversation with someone whose advice would help you determine God's intentions for you. It might start like this:**

John, what would you say if I told you I am thinking about going back to school?

Jane, you know that William and I have been dating for a long time. He seems to be getting serious. Based on what you see, do you think I should pursue this relationship?

Sue, I'm thinking about quitting. Tell me what you think.

Pastor Sam, I have had these funny feelings lately— every time I volunteer at the homeless shelter. They have an opening for an assistant director. I am wondering if...I know it sounds crazy...but if maybe God is calling me to that position. Honestly, what do you think?

Bobby, I feel awfully unsettled about my career. I'm doing what I studied to do, but I can't see myself doing it much longer. I really want to know how I can please God with my vocation. You have been in my small group for three years now. Tell me straight. What do you see me doing as a career?

A conversation like that might be just what you need as you seek to find and do what God cut you out for. Of course that conversation must be with someone who will be frank with you, and whose opinion you value.

Richard Foster, in his book *Celebration of Discipline*, even suggested what may be called "meetings for clearness." Foster described a young man who had sought answers for his life's direction through a number of avenues, including vocational tests and guidance courses. When he still did not sense a word from the Lord, he called together a group of Christian friends who worshipped with him, gave him honest feedback, and discussed his possibilities. Through the support of that group, the young man found his place in God's plan.

M—Motive

A few years ago, when I was thinking and praying about coming to Bon Air Baptist as pastor, I met regularly with a great friend, John Luckett. John constantly asked me tough questions. "Why do you really want to go?" he'd ask. He probed into my motivation. "Is it the size of the church? The prestige of the position? Why would you leave the church you love to go to Richmond?"

John cares enough about me to hold me accountable. He knows that a human can rationalize anything. We can play mind games with ourselves and even convince our-selves that our motives are pure when, in fact, we are being very self-absorbed.

For example, in the tenth grade I found myself sitting the bench on the football team, just watching the other players play. In the ninth grade I was left guard; in the tenth grade I was left *out*. I could have sat there on the bench, content to get in the game from time to time (like when we were ahead 50 to 0) and make a contribution to the team in practice. I was too proud to do that, however. I decided I would quit.

It would have been embarrassing just to walk into the coach's office and throw in the towel, so I put a spiritual spin on it. I engaged in some fancy rationalization; I convinced myself that God was telling me to quit. So I marched into the coach's office and announced that I felt it was God's will for me to leave the team.

The coach was not a religious man and made no attempt to appear so. But his response has remained with me to this day. After a dramatic pause, he replied, "Son, I'm sure you know a lot more about that kind of thing than I do. But I wouldn't want us to blame something on God that He didn't have anything to do with." I don't recall my response. I probably mumbled something dim-witted and slithered out the door.

Coach was right. I had taken a serious and holy con-cept—the concept that the Creator of the world has a plan for me—and had adulterated it by using the term *God's will* to justify my own choice. Needless to say, my motives for claiming to know God's desires were not pure.

Unfortunately, a number of us misuse this concept of the will of God. **We sometimes appeal to God's will to defend our decisions or to avoid responsibility for our actions.**

("God told me...," for example, is a common claim, and hard to refute!) Often this is not a premeditated decision on our part; we probably are not going to deceive ourselves and others intentionally. Rationalization is unusually dangerous because it typically is an unconscious reality.

Of course, the fact that the will of God is abused or exploited by people with wrong motives does not nullify its importance. People counterfeit money all the time, but that doesn't negate the value of the real stuff. Don't let someone else's misuse of the concept of God's will rob you of the joy of living out your call. More importantly, **you and I have to be cognizant of our own motives, and self-aware enough to realize that if we aren't careful, we can convince ourselves that something is God's will when He might prefer not to be associated with our decision.**

The fact that we *want* to do something certainly can be an indication that God created us to do it. However, we have to be honest with ourselves about *why* we want to do it. Right motives are critical.

There are only two ways that I know of to check our motives. The first is sincere, God-aided introspection. David prayed, *"Search me, O God, and know my heart.... And see if there be any wicked way in me"* (Psalm 139:23, 24 KJV). Earnest prayer that God will help us see our true motives is critical. A second means of determining our true motives is to find spiritually mature people who care enough about us to shoot straight with us. An accountability partner (like my friend John) can help us see what we cannot see on our own.

If our motivation is not as pure as humanly possible, then our judgment is impaired. Mixed motives muddle our musings. We can easily ignore the input of God's Spirit. We can mistake our selfish desires for a word from the Lord. By doing so we might jump unwisely into places where we don't belong, or leave places where we ought to stay. Furthermore, selfish intentions jeopardize the ultimate reward for our service.

The Bible tells us, *"Therefore judge nothing before the appointed time; wait till the Lord comes. He will bring to light what is hidden in darkness and will expose the motives of men's hearts. At that time each will receive his praise from God"* (1 Corinthians 4:5). One day we will stand before our Maker, and He will expose whether we have done good to get credit, or because doing good grew out of who we are. He will expose whether or not we've sought our own glory or His. **Let's live so that when God says, *"Well done, good and faithful servant,"* He will be able to add, "and you did it for the right reasons."**

P—Peculiar Passions

"For it is God who works in you to will and to act according to his good purpose" (Philippians 2:13). Your peculiarities are what make you, you. There are unique aspects of your makeup which, when explored, can help you determine God's call. **When you take a look at those things about which you are passionate—peculiarly passionate—you will begin to see God's call unfold.**

Near the end of the workday Ralph can hardly contain his enthusiasm. "I can't wait till tonight," he exclaims to his co-worker.

"What's the big deal about tonight?" his co-worker inquires.

Ralph exclaims, "Tonight is the night of the children's English-as-a-second-language class that I teach at the church. Tonight is 'bring a dish from your country' night!"

"Let me get this straight," says his co-worker. "You get all excited about sitting around with kids who speak very little English and whose customs are different from ours. And tonight you're going to eat weird food. You actually like that?"

"I *love* it," answers Ralph. "Wouldn't *everybody* love that?"

Well, no, as wonderful as it sounds to some people, not *everybody* would love it. Some people would wonder how Ralph has the energy to do that at the end of a long day. The fact that Ralph loves children who speak another language is one of his peculiar passions. And that distinctive characteristic of his makeup lets us know that he is probably living out his calling in that English-as-a-second-language class.

So what are your peculiar passions? What do *you* love to do that some folks think is downright crazy? What are the issues and who are the people you care about most deeply, but that seem humdrum or even loathsome to others? Which situations turn you on and turn some people off? What opportunities stoke your fire and make some people yawn? Your peculiar passions are God-given, and God didn't give them to you to waste.

It is indeed necessary to surrender our wills to God's will. However, we don't have to be afraid when we do that. God's call will align with the way He created us. He is too wise to cut you out for one role and then force you into another. His call comes at the intersection of who you are with what the world needs. God's call will point you to where your gifts and passions overlap with humanity's hardships. So you not only get to make a contribution, you get to have a good time doing it!

It is God Himself who created the good desires of your heart. It is not absurd, then, to think that what you really would *like* to do is actually what God really would like for you to do!

I love what I do. Even when I was a little boy, I used to come home from church and stand at our coffee table and preach. I'd try to remember the words the pastor had used that morning. I remember using the King James Version phrase, "Verily, verily," a lot. I didn't know what "verily" meant, but it sounded very ministerial!

I almost always would give an invitation to accept Jesus, or an altar call. My mother would come from the kitchen where she was preparing Sunday lunch, and my Dad would get up out of his easy chair to respond to my altar call. (My mom and dad hold the world record for conversion experiences.)

Years later, when I was 20 years old, I was sitting with a pastor and his wife at Sunday lunch when I commented, "There is a part of me that would really enjoy being a pastor, but that's not what I'm going to do." He replied, "Wanting to be a pastor is not natural. You'd better be careful; that might be what God will call you to be." He was right; God did call me to the pastorate. And as simplistic as it sounds, it "feels right."

When I was invited to become the pastor at Bon Air Baptist Church it "felt right." First, it was a call to be a pastor; but there's more than that. When my wife and I went to Nigeria as missionaries in 1991, we assumed we would be in that role until our retirement. Since before we were married, Keri and I had planned for missionary service. Then, when we were on one-year stateside assignment (formerly called furlough), my father suffered a stroke. The stroke was debilitating for him, and eventually took his life. Because I am an only child, we remained in the States to take care of my mother.

We are still missionaries at heart, however, and Bon Air Baptist Church fulfills our great desire to be involved in missions. Ours is a church that is fervently involved in global and local missions—going, giving, and sending missionaries at a level that few churches reach. In these and other ways, this particular church is the fulfillment of many of my God-given dreams.

I love the way Max Lucado puts it in *Cure for the Common Life*. He declares that everybody has a "sweet spot":

> What engineers give sports equipment, God gave you. A zone, a region, a life precinct in which you were made to dwell. He tailored the curves of your life to fit an empty space in his jigsaw puzzle. And life makes sweet sense when you find your spot.

I truly have found my sweet spot. I believe I was created to be right where I am, doing exactly what I am doing. It wasn't my first choice (my wife and I wanted to be missionaries until we retired). And it isn't without its difficulties. But I feel like I am, as some athletes would say, "in the zone." Lucado describes the sweet spot further as "where *what* you do (your unique giftedness) intersects with *why* you do it (making a big deal out of God) and *where* you do it (every day of your life)." That's it for me. At this point in my life, the confluence of the what, why, and where gives me a deep sense of rightness.

What would be *your* sweet spot? What are the good and noble desires of *your* heart? What are your dreams, your passions? Sometimes what *feels* right, *is* right. What we feel is certainly not the only criterion for making a decision, for our feelings can be selfish and prideful. But following the good and noble desires of our hearts is a good beginning.

So, again, what are the things about which you feel passionately? What issues stir your heart? To what group of people do you feel most drawn? What area of need would you really like to address? If you could do any kind of service that you pleased, what would that be? What makes you think, "Wow, if I could do that, they wouldn't have to call me to remind me when the next meeting or event is"?

Where does your personality best suit you to serve? With people? Coordinating programs? Where everything is orderly? Where chaos is normal? Would you rather start something new or maintain and improve something in existence? Are you an extrovert or an introvert? Do you have the gift of leadership or do you prefer to follow?

Your answers might just tell you what God is calling you to do. *Enthusiasm* is a combination of two Greek words: *en* (in), and *theos* (God). Enthusiasm, then, is that passion that God places in us. Follow your enthusiasm, and you will be well on the way to finding your God-given call.

Does this mean we will be thrilled with everything we do within God's call? Of course not. Yet even tedious acts take on significance when they fall within the Creator's instructions for us.

A—Aptitudes

> *"Each one should use whatever gift he has received to serve others, faithfully administering God's grace in its various forms....If anyone serves, he should do it with the strength God provides" (1 Peter 4:10, 11).*

> *"To one he gave five talents of money, to another two talents, and to another one talent, each according to his ability" (Matthew 25:15).*

> *"Each person is given something to do that shows who God is: Everyone gets in on it, everyone benefits. All kinds of things are handed out by the Spirit, and to all kinds of people!" (1 Corinthians 12:7 The Message).*

"The body we're talking about is Christ's body of chosen people. Each of us finds our meaning and function as a part of his body. But as a chopped-off finger or cut-off toe we wouldn't amount to much, would we? So since we find ourselves fashioned into all these excellently formed and marvelously functioning parts in Christ's body, let's just go ahead and be what we were made to be, without enviously or pridefully comparing ourselves with each other, or trying to be something we aren't" (Romans 12:5–6 The Message).

God didn't create the wind and tell it to provide shade. God created wind to provide breezes. God didn't create the water and tell it to warm His people. God created water to provide cooling and to provide life-giving refreshment to His people. He created individual elements of His creation for specific duties and wants them to serve their function. Why would He be any less intentional about us? **Why would God create us with unique aptitudes and expect us to do something that didn't fit?**

Each person born into God's family through faith in Jesus has at least one spiritual gift. The gifts are listed in various places in the New Testament, including Romans and 1 Corinthians. There are a lot of books and classes available to help you discover how God has uniquely gifted you. Ideas about how to compile and formulate a list of spiritual gifts vary, but Bruce Bugbee, Don Cousins, and Bill Hybels, in their book *Network*, have suggested the following "master list" of the gifts for us:

GIFTS

Administration	Intercession
Apostleship	Interpretation
Craftsmanship	Knowledge
Creative communication	Leadership
Discernment	Mercy
Encouragement	Miracles
Evangelism	Prophecy
Faith	Shepherding
Giving	Teaching
Healing	Tongues
Helps	Wisdom
Hospitality	

Besides spiritual gifts, you have natural abilities. Romans 12:6 from the New Living Translation (NLT) reads, *"God has given each of us the ability to do certain things well."* God's gifts to us of those "certain things" help us understand His plan for us. Don't assume that any talent you have is useless.

What are your "certain things"? The ability to maintain a building? To build a Web site? To entertain children? To comfort older adults? To read a financial statement or a musical score? To speak publicly? What are your natural abilities?

A few years ago Ron Moore, a member of our church, took me to lunch at Richmond's Strawberry Street Café. His intention was to tell me he was going to step down from one of his ministries in our church. During lunch Ron said, "I am a deacon, and honored to be one. But I just don't feel like that is my calling." "No problem," I told him, "let's find what you are called to do."

After another bite of salad from their famous bathtub salad bar I said, "By the way, a few of us are going to Illinois soon to meet with Lyle Schaller about the idea of becoming one church in multiple locations." As I talked, Ron got real interested. Ron is the guy who dreamed up CarMax for Circuit City. He is literally one of our country's leading experts in new ventures. It took me a while to put two and two together, but finally I made the connection in my mind between Ron's expertise in new ventures and our upcoming new venture. I said, "Ron, would you be interested in helping us figure out if we're supposed to do this multisite thing, and if so, how we can do it?" He signed on right there, went to Illinois with us, and is a key member of the team that led our church to launch a second campus. Ron is using his gift, and is passionate about it.

If you aren't using your gifts or skills, let someone you trust help you find where and how you can. And don't assume that spiritual gifts are to be used *only* within the church building. Remember that the church is you and your fellow Christ followers wherever you are found. You can exercise your spiritual gifts wherever you are.

S—Seasoning

Are you a new believer? A believer who, to this point, has not yet grown in your faith? Or are you a longtime believer who has continued to mature? Your answer will help determine what you should do. The Bible cautions, for example, against a new believer taking on certain roles before having the time to season a bit as a Christ follower (1 Timothy 3:1, 6). Are you maturing spiritually, and thus becoming fit for greater responsibilities? What about your experience? Have you had sufficient experience to be prepared for the opportunity you are considering?

Several years ago I asked someone I admired to recommend me to a certain position. It was a "dream" position, and I was certain that this individual's nod would put me on the inside track.

But he refused; he said I wasn't ready for it. Wasn't ready for it?! What was he thinking? Did he not look at the résumé I had sent him?

Well, the truth is that when I got over my hurt feelings I had to admit deep down that he was right. My experience was indeed inadequate for the role I was coveting. Had I gotten that position it probably would have been disastrous both for the organization and for me. I have thanked God a number of times for *not* getting that position. (I still haven't thanked the guy for not recommending me, though.) ·

There is no shame in not being ready for a certain role. The shame is in taking on something for which we needed more preparation.

On the other hand, if you are a seasoned follower of Jesus, perhaps you ought to be assuming greater responsibility within God's kingdom. Not long ago Suzy, the leader of an exercise class that I attend, asked me, "Are you adding weights every couple of weeks?" I sheepishly admitted that I was working at the same level of difficulty as when I began, several weeks earlier. I'd begun to coast.

Don't coast. If you have been a follower of Jesus for a while, then it is time to pray about bigger responsibilities. Note that I did not say larger numbers and more glamorous positions, but bigger responsibilities. In Jesus's parable of the talents, the master said to the faithful servant, *"Well done, good and faithful servant! You have been faithful with a few things; I will put you in charge of many things"* (Matthew 25:21, 23). And Paul wrote that it is a shame when people who should be enjoying steak dinners are still drinking only milk. Do your present responsibilities in the body of Christ represent an appropriate level of maturity?

It would be irresponsible of me to suggest that every call follower ought to be taking on heavier loads and more complex tasks. And I sure would not want to leave the impression that we ought to be aggressively seeking more prestigious roles. Yet to "coast"—to let our accumulating wisdom and experience go unused—doesn't seem like good stewardship of our gifts either. **A constant evaluation of where we are in our spiritual development ought to help us discern God's ongoing call.**

S—Sensible decision making

"Make a careful exploration of who you are and the work you have been given, and then sink yourself into that" (Galatians 6:4 *The Message*). This search for the will of God deserves our "careful exploration." We must not leave our brains in neutral. **When we enter the quest for God's will, we must not check our common sense and logic at the door.** We have to gather and consider all the information possible.

In every decision—"Should we move or not?" "What is the best health-care option for my ill and aging parent?" "Should I accept that invitation to serve on the board?" "Is it right for me to take that new ministry position?"—God expects us to use the common sense with which He has blessed us. Common sense is not enough by itself. In fact, our human reasoning can mislead us. But common sense is important to the process.

One means of exercising good sense in considering a call is to "try it on." I was visiting one night with two career missionaries. Several months earlier, walking across a street in Caracas, I had experienced God's call to be a missionary. The sense that God had prepared and prompted me to be an international missionary could not have been more real. Now the question was, "What kind of missionary should I be? A social worker? A campus minister? A teacher?" I never had preached a sermon, but I was beginning to wonder if God was calling me to be a "regular" missionary—the kind that preaches and plants churches.

Joe Powell was one of the other missionaries in the room that night. Hoping he hadn't gone to sleep, I asked, "Joe, how did you know God was calling you to preach?" Joe didn't respond with an explanation; he responded with an invitation. "I tell you what," he said. "Why don't you come to Faith some Sunday and preach in the English service?" (Joe was the pastor of Faith Baptist Church in Maracaibo— a church with an English service and a Spanish service.)

I took him up on it, and a few weeks later I was standing in the pulpit of Faith Baptist Church. It's hard to explain, but as soon as the service was over I knew, I just knew, that God had cut me out to preach. I certainly had not produced a sermonic masterpiece; but it was like trying on a suit that fit.

A lot of people have found their place in the body of Christ by simply "trying on" ministries that seemed compelling. Many have tried on a ministry and sensed immediately that it was a good fit. Others, however, have wondered, "What was I thinking?" (If you are going to try on a ministry, you must go into it with a willingness to admit it if it isn't right for you, and the leaders of that ministry must understand that you aren't obligated to continue if it doesn't work out.)

This approach is certainly advantageous if you are considering a volunteer ministry. From teaching two-year-olds in Sunday School to helping out at a homeless shelter, trying it on can help you find your function(s) in the body of Christ. Trying it on is even applicable to vocational ministry. For example, at our church in Richmond we have some young adults taking on different ministry roles. They believe they know what God is calling them to do, and we are helping them to confirm that call before they set out on a career path. A lot of missionary-sending agencies are even encouraging people to go overseas on short-term (six-month) assignments before they make a commitment to career missions.

Of course, I don't advise anyone with a family to quit your job, get another degree, and take a completely new career path just to try it on. If you can test the waters without undue risk, however, that should help you discern God's will for you.

You must remember that this is not a selfish pursuit; you are seeking God's plan for you. When I suggest that we try on something, I am not suggesting a lukewarm commitment to God's leadership. I'm not talking about hedging our bets. I do understand, however, that discerning the will of God is a mysterious venture. Research is a means of using our God-given good sense in exploring our call. "Trying on" a call is, to quote Galatians 6:4 again, a way to "make a careful exploration of who you are and the work you have been given." If it fits, you then can "sink yourself into that."

Another way to look at things sensibly is to do an autobiography. Look back on your life. Someone has said that God's will is best understood in retrospect. Søren Kierkegaard is credited with saying, "Life must be understood backwards; but...it must be lived forward." We often can look back and see God at work—orchestrating events to bring us to a certain point. What you see in your rearview mirror just might reveal what God wants for you down the road.

What experiences have you had that would enable you to contribute to the body of Christ? What have been your vocational or personal experiences? Even your negative experiences prepare you for service. Did that job that once seemed like a waste of time now appear to have prepared you for unique ministry? Did the family environment in which you grew up help you to understand and fit into certain human situations in which some people are uncomfortable? For what has life prepared you?

Can you remember specific times when you felt God's pleasure? Is there a time when everything converged and you felt like you were in a groove, in your "sweet spot"? If so, then that is a good indication of God's intention for your life. So look back through your personal history. Your own autobiography will help you interpret the present promptings of God's Spirit; it will help you make a sensible decision.

These directional indicators, which I present to you as a COMPASS for your life, have been helpful to me as I have explored what I believe to be God's promptings in my own life. In doing so, I have found it necessary to give a balanced emphasis to each of the different indicators. In other words, I cannot follow my passions without balancing those passions with the observations of others, a sincere assessment of my motives, and so on. I cannot go by my aptitudes without balancing that with good sense, and so on. Each of the elements of the COMPASS is important.

Obviously this tool must be covered and supported by prayer. No human tool can supplant the mystical work of God's Spirit communing with our spirit. I pray that, as you sincerely seek to discern and follow God's call, the COMPASS will be a helpful tool.

LET'S NOT MAKE IT HARDER THAN IT HAS TO BE

4

Jesus's invitation often was a simple, "Follow Me." That's a pretty straightforward appeal. Maybe we have made the call more complicated than God intended it to be.

After asking you to work through the COMPASS, I now want to take the pressure off a bit. It is indeed important that we take seriously the discerning of God's call. Sometimes, however, I think that we make understanding His call more complicated than God intends it to be. **God's grace gives us some breathing room.**

Don't be bound by the assumption that there is only one decision that you can make and still be within God's plan for you.

Our daughter, Brennan, was about 14 when she told me she was diligently seeking God's will regarding the college she would attend. I told her I was glad to hear of her desire to follow God's purposes for her, and asked if there had been anything in particular that had sparked this quest for the right college. "I probably will meet my husband at college," she said. "And if I go to the wrong college, then I won't meet the one God wants me to marry!"

Hmmm. Interesting concept.

I suggested to her that God might be pleased with any number of college choices she could make. And I even hinted that there might be more than one male that is "within God's will" for her.

She seemed relieved.

I don't think the will of God for one's life is limited to that *one* job or that *one* place where one could live or that *one* role in God's kingdom that one could fulfill. My understanding of God's will is that He wants me to long for the fulfillment of His purposes for humankind, and to find where I fit into that picture. And there might be more than one role where I could fit.

Let's consider a possible scenario. A deeply devoted, 22-year-old follower of Jesus is graduating with a bachelor of science in nursing. She has four job offers. Is there only *one* of those positions that is in God's will for her? Maybe. Maybe not.

Certainly she is going to pray and ask for God's direction. She is going to consult those whose counsel she trusts. And she is going to ask the following questions about those potential places of employment:

- *Is there one place that seems to fit my skills best?*
- *Is there one place where the needs are greatest?*
- *Is there one place where I will be able to reach my God-given potential?*
- *Are my motives appropriate for a follower of Jesus? In other words, is this decision about how best I can*

> serve God and humankind, or is this purely about what's in it for me?

I believe God gives us the freedom to make choices. I believe that as long as her motives are Christlike and her intentions are pure—as long as she does the best she can do, and what she chooses is consistent with God's mission and His character—God will be delighted with whichever decision she makes. A desire to follow God's call is the most important aspect of this quest.

If we concentrate on being who God wants us to be, then doing what He wants us to do will come naturally.

We become who God created us to be by practicing spiritual disciplines. The disciplines shape our hearts. The practice of the disciplines will make a "formula" less necessary in our quest to do God's will. So read the Bible faithfully. Pray without ceasing. Fast on those occasions when you long for a particularly close relationship with God. Read good books. And practice solitude. Solitude is so important (and so uncommon) I want to spend a little extra time here.

Jesus returned time and again to the practice of solitude. Often Jesus got away to be alone with the Father for extended periods of time. Jesus knew that it is much easier to hear the voice of the Father in quiet solitude than in the middle of a noisy, busy day.

Dallas Willard noted, in *The Spirit of the Disciplines*, that solitary confinement is used in prisons as a means of breaking prisoners' wills by getting them away from interaction with other humans. Likewise, solitude—getting away from our daily hubbub—can shape our wills, and, if necessary, *break* our wills, by forcing us to look inward and upward, instead of outward at the many distractions of our fast-paced lives.

Find a time and place to get away with nothing but your Bible. If you are really disciplined, take an entire day. If you want to ease into it, just take a morning. But you don't have to get away every time you want solitude. I've found that the simple discipline of turning off the car radio is good from time to time.

Solitude is about being still and knowing that God is God. I'm talking about living the words of the hymn "In the Garden": "He walks with me, and He talks with me." The hymn, by the way, doesn't say, "He works with me, and He shops with me, and He calls me on my cell phone!" He walks with us and talks with us most intimately when we choose to be still and know that He is God. If you will practice solitude, perhaps you can say with the hymn, "And the joy we share as we tarry there, none other has ever known."

In this quest to hear God's call, nothing can take the place of quiet before our Creator. Calvin Miller wrote, in *The Empowered Leader:*

> God does not shout His best vision through hassled Christian living. It is in the quiet that He gives His most delivering visions of life....Perhaps in the cathedral of the trees, under the silence of the stars, or by the moaning sea, you'll be most likely to see the true light and hear the "still, small voice."

Finally, remember that we serve a God of grace.

Sharron sensed a clear call to be a missionary to Africa during a spiritual retreat in college. Soon after that, however, she met a handsome, charming baseball player who stole her heart and, in a sense, stole her call. The two were married and now, two decades and two kids later, Sharron squirms while the guest speaker in her church—a missionary from Africa—pleads with people to join him and his colleagues in international mission service. "Don't just pay and pray!" he pleads. "Some of you should go!" Sharron's mind goes back to that college retreat during which she told her campus minister that she was called to be a missionary to Africa. She feels ashamed that she abandoned that call.

So has Sharron blown it completely? Has God turned His back on her? Certainly not.

There will be opportunities to serve as a volunteer overseas, perhaps after retirement. Yet Sharron doesn't have to wait for that. God meets us where we are and invites us to walk with Him from that point—even those who blew an original call to missions. God was right there with Jonah in the belly of a big fish, and with John Mark back in Jerusalem after he'd left Paul and Barnabas high and dry in Pamphylia.

God has accomplished some wonderful things through people who missed, or even abandoned, their original calls. People who have wandered off course still can use their compass. That is what Sharron will do; she will consult her COMPASS. She will ask:

- What is that recurring prompting of God's Spirit?
- What are others observing about me?

- Are my motives pure or am I just trying to work off the guilt of not being a missionary all those years ago?
- What are my peculiar passions?
- What are my aptitudes, and in what areas might God want to use them?
- How is my seasoning—my level of spiritual maturity and my experience—going to determine the role in which I serve?
- What makes sense? I have a family to consider, so how can I lovingly fulfill my responsibility to my family *and* find a place in service of God and His people?

Sharron will find that God specializes in second chances. She can serve as a short-term missions volunteer, in a Christian homeless ministry, or in helping her church start a new congregation. She won't view those as chances to make up for a mistake; she will see them as opportunities to join God on mission *now*, regardless of the past.

When (not *if*) we make an honest mistake in judgment, God does not write us off. Most of us probably could look back without much of a strain and remember times when we made poor decisions, and yet God salvaged the situation. The Bible would be a thin book if we removed all the stories of God rescuing His people from their blunders. Obviously that does not give us license for a cavalier attitude regarding His will for us. It does, however, remind us that **His grace is amazing, even when our judgment is amazingly bad.** That, more than anything, takes the pressure off—when no formula offers a guarantee.

DON'T LET OBSTACLES STOP YOU

5

Does the possession of a COMPASS ensure an obstacle-free journey? Well, what do you think Lewis and Clark would say to that?

From time to time I hear people say, "It must be the will of God, for everything has just fallen into place." I get a little nervous when I hear that, for sometimes missional living is messy. Sometimes the path to a God-given ministry opportunity is a circuitous one. Sometimes there are logs across the path and dangerous curves in the road. **Obstacles are not necessarily indications that God is in opposition to what is happening. Likewise, the absence of obstacles is not necessarily a sign of God's blessing or approval.**

Warren Wiersbe noted, in *Be Amazed,* that if Jonah had followed only the circumstances, the "open doors," he might well have concluded that God was calling him *away from* Nineveh. After all, everything seemed to fall into place! When he got to the docks at Joppa, the ship was right there waiting for him! He just happened to have enough money for a ticket! And he had such a peace about things that he was able to sleep during a storm! Wiersbe concluded, "It's possible to be out of the will of God and still have circumstances appear to be working on your behalf."

The Bible says that if we trust the Lord, instead of our own understanding, God will make our paths straight (Proverbs 3:5–6). I think some of us have interpreted this verse to mean that if we find God's will—if we follow His call—then everything will line up perfectly. Perhaps some of us look for smooth sailing as a confirmation that we are truly doing what God wants us to do. But the Bible is filled with evidence to the contrary. Scripture and Christian history tell us that a lot of folks have suffered a lot of resistance while following God's call.

Let me offer an example from our church of how obstacles can be misleading. For three years our church did a lot of talking and planning and praying about a multisite ministry—becoming a church in multiple locations. There arose a consensus among church leaders that one of our roles in God's mission was to add worship sites for our church in locations beyond the original campus, and the congregation voted to do that. But a few months after our decision—about five months before we were supposed to launch our first new site—circumstances were not encouraging.

We couldn't find a site in the area we wanted to begin our new location; we couldn't find anywhere to meet. We couldn't find a building to lease that had the right square footage except in places where the price was out of our range. Our request to use a local high school that we thought would provide a great location was denied. Circumstances seemed to say that we weren't supposed to be doing this multisite thing; we could have assumed God was closing the door and abandoned the vision.

Yet there was a deep sense among our leaders that we were pursuing the right course, so we pressed on. Then things began to happen. We found a marvelous "site pastor" and a great staff for the new location. A lot of remarkable folks, strong leaders in our church, emerged who said they had been called to be part of a launch team. Then the high school officials reversed their decision and said we could come. Besides that, the new person in charge of the facility at the school is a Christian and a member of a church that meets in two locations, so he understands the multisite idea and is helping us succeed!

If we had been sitting there a month from the projected launch without a place to meet, without a staff, and without volunteers, we probably would have been right in rethinking our decision to become a multisite church. Obstacles, after all, are not to be ignored. They must, however, be weighed alongside other indications. Had we considered only the obstacles, I believe we would have missed an opportunity to fulfill one of our roles in God's mission.

God does not always orchestrate everything according to our calendar or strategy. Things don't always go according to plan. Circumstances, when considered alongside other indications, can be helpful in discerning God's voice; but not everything falls perfectly into place—even when God is calling.

On the other hand, God does close doors now and then. There are times when we are headed down a wrong path, and God steps in to prevent our getting too far off course. When we keep banging our heads against the wall and God doesn't seem to be intervening, it is time to consider whether the obstacles might have been placed there by God. In other words...

Don't whip the donkey. In the Old Testament Book of Numbers we find Balaam riding his donkey on a mission. But, alas, his mission was interrupted by the inexplicable stubbornness of Balaam's beast of burden. The donkey refused to proceed. Balaam was beating the donkey when the donkey said, in Hebrew, "Hey, dude, what's up with that?" (OK, that's a rough translation.)

Then God allowed Balaam to see what the donkey had been seeing, and which had been invisible to Balaam, an angel with an attitude was standing in the road with his sword drawn. If Balaam had continued, he would have been in big trouble. But the stubborn donkey prevented his going farther.

Laurie Beth Jones, author of *Jesus CEO*, used that story to make a wonderful point: sometimes God places obstructions in our paths for our own good. Those things that prevent us from moving ahead might be there for our protection. Sometimes God closes the door because He knows what is beyond it isn't good for us, or so that He can open another door to something better.

When our oldest son, Landon, was looking at colleges, I wanted Landon to get into a particular university. Landon had said that he sensed God was calling him into some sort of vocational ministry and, of course, I wanted him to get the best possible preparation for that. Believing that this particular university would be best for him, I prayed. I even fasted. I did a prayerwalk—I went to the campus, walked around on it, and prayed over it.

But Landon didn't get in.

He did, however, get into Christopher Newport University (CNU), a great school. CNU has turned out to be the place I believe with all my heart God wanted for Landon. The

Leadership School, his friends, his church, even his relationship with the president and his wife—it's just what Landon needed. As it turns out, God is smarter than I am! God didn't give me what I prayed for, but He gave me what I prayed for.

Obstacles are not always indications that God is opposing our undertakings. Yet if we have prayed and worked and prayed and worked and God still does not remove the barrier, we can assume it is there for a divine reason...so don't whip the donkey.

Don't wait until you have all the answers. Life would be much less stressful if decisions were easy. How wonderful it would be if the difference between good and bad, or better and best, were always clear cut. But they're not. I do not believe that God always signals His pleasure by making our decisions easy. Often making a decision requires a leap—or at least a step—of faith.

One evening I was officiating a football game between two local high schools. A runner came my way and I followed him down the sideline, glancing from side to side looking for holds or clips or other potential fouls. My primary responsibility, however, was the runner and the ball.

When the runner was tackled, several yards downfield, I saw right where he fell. There was only one problem; he had fallen with his back toward me, and when he rolled over, he didn't have the ball! He had been running with it, but he no longer possessed it. I looked back about five yards and there was a player from the other team with the ball in his hand! It was obvious the runner didn't have it when he hit the ground, but I had no idea how the other player had gotten it.

A second official arrived on the scene and I asked him, "Did you see what happened?" He hadn't. But we reasoned that the only thing that could have happened was that the runner was stripped of the ball before he fell, back around the spot where the player from the other team stood holding the ball. It was the only thing that made sense.

So I made a call. I called it defense's ball, first down, at the spot where the player was holding it. (The young man who'd been carrying the ball didn't complain, so I figured we probably had gotten it right.) Well, the fans went berserk. The coach went berserk*er*! I looked a bit like I didn't know what I was doing, I'll admit. And I had to make a decision based on insufficient information. But I had to make a decision.

Someone said, "Not to decide is to decide." Someone else said, "He who hesitates is lost."

Franklin Delano Roosevelt was warned by his staff that his plans to end the Depression were too large, too costly, and too rough. "Well," he thundered, "maybe they aren't perfect in every way. But we've got to do something!" His administration is credited with putting this country back on its feet again. All because one leader was bold enough to make a decision based on the limited information at his disposal.

I said all that to say that you won't always be able to know everything you would like to know before making a decision. You will pray and do your research. You will consult your COMPASS. Yet you still might not have the kind of certainty you would like. At that point you have to do the best you can to follow your call, with limited information.

Ecclesiastes 11:4 tells us: *"Whoever watches the wind will not plant; whoever looks at the clouds will not reap."* Former President Jimmy Carter wrote about those verses in

Sources off Strength. He noted that they sound like bad advice for farmers, for farmers know that they must pay attention to the weather. President Carter wrote that a farmer has to watch the weather, of course, but noted that if the farmer obsesses over the humidity and the temperature and the soil conditions, and if he fixates on the advice of every so-called expert in the county, he might never feel the time is right to plant. He might always be thinking the conditions will be better tomorrow. And before the farmer knows it, the time for sowing will have passed. So it is with decisions.

Decisions always will be somewhat subjective. My personal experience is that I make most of my decisions based on the best I can understand of my own gifts and desires, the circumstances, the advice of people who love me, and the best I can determine about what God wants. There always is, however, an element of faith.

I mentioned Ron Moore earlier. Ron happens to be the brains behind CarMax, the wildly successful used car company. Ron is a business consultant and came up with the CarMax idea for Circuit City a few years ago. He is skilled at designing innovative enterprises and getting them successfully off the ground. His consulting company is called Fidía. Fidía stands for Forget It and Do It Anyway. **Yes, there comes a time when you've just got to *do it.***

That's not to say that Ron is slack in doing his homework. He gives well-researched advice to his business clients. In our new ventures at the church he forces us to think through things very thoroughly. I love him for that because he makes me consider all sides of an issue. Yet Ron knows that there comes a time when you have gathered all the information that you can reasonably gather. A few more tidbits won't help. And nobody ever knows everything about anything. There comes a point when you've just got to "fish or cut bait." You've got to take the proverbial plunge. You've got to forget it and do it anyway.

Remember that the call comes to people with imperfect pasts. If you think God only calls people with pristine personal histories, you've got another think coming. Some take the bumpy and indirect route to a volunteer or vocational ministry position. Remember Moses.

Moses' first 40 years were spent in the lap of luxury, as a fair-haired member of the first family, a privileged prince in a palace. Then one day he stood watching the hard labor of the Hebrew people, whom he somehow had come to recognize as *his* people. They were slavishly building Pharaoh's buildings and farming Pharaoh's farms. Moses' blood boiled and his pulse raced as he watched an Egyptian taskmaster beating a Hebrew slave. The passion of his roots took over and Moses jumped the Egyptian overseer. The killing was not premeditated; Moses acted out of rage. But the Egyptian ended up just as dead as if Moses had planned it.

Moses fled. He went
- from extravagance to exile,
- from the harem to the herd,
- from luxury to labor.

Moses fled and he fled and he fled until he ended up in Midian, a dust bowl of a place in the southeastern Sinai desert. Moses lived every day with the painful reality that he was an alien—a stranger in a strange place. An outsider. A prince turned migrant worker. A fugitive in a foreign land.

Moses seemed destined to spend his life as a second-class citizen in a second-rate country.

But God was using that difficult period to prepare Moses for the most important event in Israel's history. You see, Moses *needed* those dark days. As a pampered product of Pharaoh's palace he was not ready for the rigors of leading the Hebrews out of Egypt. Moses needed the crucible of Midian to refine him, to prepare him for the task ahead.

We all have our Midians. **On at least one page in the passport of each life, in bold letters, is stamped, *Midian.*** All of us should have T-shirts with the words: *Been to Midian.* We all experience the dark, disheartening days of our personal crucibles.

Everyone passes through difficulties; but we are affected by them differently. Some of us *respond* to adversity and emerge *better* for it; others *react* to adversity and emerge *bitter* for it. Some of us come out stronger, with deeper faith. Others come out weaker, with shaken faith. What is the difference? At least one difference is the way we choose to allow our adversity to have an impact on us.

There are some things over which we have no control. But we can determine whether or not we will emerge from our trials better or bitter, and whether or not we will allow God to shape us and strengthen us through the difficulties and prepare us for greater challenges.

Moses was being shaped and strengthened in Midian. We don't hear anything from him for four decades. Then, one day, when Moses was about 80 years old, he saw a burning bush—a bush burning with a flame fueled by God Himself. He saw some divine pyrotechnics.

God proclaimed from the bush, "I have heard the cries of my people and am concerned about their suffering." (When you think no one hears your cries, by the way, God does.) And God called Moses from leading sheep to leading Israelites out of Egypt. Moses returned

- from exile to exodus,
- from herdsman of his father-in-law's sheep
  to helmsman of his nation's ship,
- from lawbreaker to lawgiver.

In short, God *redeemed* Moses' past.

What do you think of when you hear the word *redeem*? I often think of the Green Stamp store. Before I started school, and sometimes in the summers after that, I'd accompany Mom to the grocery store. As she checked out she'd get a number of green stamps, depending on the amount she had purchased. Then, from time to time, I'd go with my mom to the "redemption center" where she would turn in her green stamps for toasters and lamps and so on. They called that "redeeming" the green stamps.

To "redeem" those green stamps was to exchange little, nearly worthless pieces of paper—maybe dirty from having been on the floor, or wrinkled from having been stuffed down into her purse—for something of value. God's redeeming your past means His taking something that might seem worthless to you and turning it into something very good.

Maybe you saw the movie *My Big Fat Greek Wedding.* The daughter is about to get married, and not long before the wedding she is an emotional wreck, lamenting that her family is crazy! Her brother says to her what some of us need to hear: *"Don't let your past dictate who you are, but let it be part of who you will become."* That is important advice for anyone, even if you don't have a flawless history. Don't disqualify yourself from service just because you made some bad choices along the way. God does not call only perfect folks. If He did, He would have a very small circle of associates.

Remember that the call comes to people in midcareer. If we are not careful, we will assume that if God is going to call someone to a unique role He will do so while the individual is a teenager, or maybe in college. Therefore, we assume that if we are past the age of 22, God won't tap us for anything that would require a life change for us. We assume that since it all didn't fall into place before now, it won't fall into place at all. That is a wrong assumption.

Os Guinness, in *The Call,* made the intriguing observation that a "midlife crisis" might turn out to be the very thing that opens us up to hearing the call of God! Yet even if your midlife is not in crisis, you can't assume that God is not going to "mess with" your life. The US military has a maximum age beyond which you cannot be drafted. God has no such limitations.

Back to Moses' story. At the age of 80, Moses confronted the Pharaoh. At the age of 80, he organized the Exodus, led the Israelites across the Red Sea, and for the next 40 years he held them together during the long sojourn in the wilderness— a task that turned out to strongly resemble cat herding.

Moses made his greatest contribution between the ages of 80 and 120. Based on the average life span today, I'd say that would be roughly between the ages of 50 and 80. Moses didn't drop anchor at age 80; he set sail! When others his age were reminiscing about the good old days, Moses was dreaming of the future.

I want to ask a question specifically for those of us who aren't exactly teenagers anymore: Are we willing for God to do something different in our lives—to give us a new assignment? Openness to God's leadership is not just for teenagers.

Carol Spears has been my wife's best friend since elementary school. She is now a physician who spends a great deal of her time in Africa. Her ultimate goal is to be a full-time medical missionary. Carol's decision to study medicine came in midcareer, during her visit with us while we were missionaries in Nigeria. At the time she had an upper-level management position with a large corporation. While in Nigeria on her two visits with us, she often joined missionary physicians in surgery at the Baptist hospital in Ogbomosho. Then one night at our dinner table in Nigeria, she told us she felt God was calling her to go into medicine.

Carol wasn't as old as Moses was when he saw the burning bush, but in midcareer many of us would not have considered the possibility that we could follow God's leadership into such a radical new direction for our lives. Several people on the staff of the church where I serve as pastor left secular careers to come on staff at the church. I'm fairly certain they all took significant pay cuts to do that. And I'm fairly certain a lot of folks called them crazy! Yet they all seem delighted to have followed God's call.

Some of the rest of us need to be open—like Moses and Carol were—to burning bushes. Even in midcareer! Increasingly, followers of Jesus seem open to a refreshing call from God in their 30s and 50s and 70s. Some call this the "second journey." **People are resigning, retiring, retraining, refocusing, retooling, regrouping, and receiving a fresh word from the Almighty.** They are catching their second wind—and it is the wind of God's Spirit. These new beginnings are launched with a depth of character that comes from experience that people didn't have when they were 21.

Are you open to a fresh word from God about your life—a second journey?

Remember that the call comes to unworthy people. Surely someone is thinking, "God couldn't call *me*. Not *me*, with all my quirks and limitations and all those blemishes on my record. It didn't fall into place for me because I botched things up with bad choices." If you are the one thinking that (I knew there was someone), perhaps you haven't been taking the Bible seriously. Take a quick survey of Hebrews 11, sometimes called God's hall of fame, if you don't think God calls unworthy people.

I *know* God calls unworthy people because I *am* one. I get my priorities out of order and I act selfishly and sometimes my motives are not pure. There have been points in my life when I was so insecure that I lived like the proverbial chameleon, the lizard that changes colors depending on its surroundings. With one group I thought and acted and talked one way; with another group I thought and talked and acted another way. My insecurities were so deep that my convictions were shallow. I'm a child of God who *still* makes sinful choices more often than I'd like to admit.

God, however, is grace-full. He has given me second chances.

I always have loved the New Testament story of John Mark. He got off to a bad start as a young man; he abandoned Paul and Barnabas on their missionary journey and was the reason behind the split-up of that great missionary duo. But Mark became a hero of the faith—a wonderful missionary and almost certainly the writer of one of our Gospels. Paul even asked for Mark to visit him when Paul knew his end was drawing near. Mark's story is a story of God's grace and thus I always have loved it.

One of my theme verses is 2 Corinthians 4:1: "Therefore, since through God's mercy we have this ministry, we do not lose heart." It would be easy for me to get discouraged, for I am both skillfully inadequate and personally unworthy to join God in His amazing plan for the world. Yet this verse reminds me that the calling God gave me is purely a gift of mercy. Therefore, I do not lose heart.

Don't be disheartened by the regret of past decisions. God uses unworthy people. When it comes to a call, He seems to *prefer* unworthy people, in fact.

Brothers, think of what you were when you were called. Not many of you were wise by human standards; not many were influential; not many were of noble birth. But God chose the foolish things of the world to shame the wise; God chose the weak things of the world to shame the strong. He chose the lowly things of this world and the despised things—and the things that are not—to nullify the things that are, so that no one may boast before him. It is because of him that you are in Christ Jesus,

*who has become for us wisdom from God—that is,
our righteousness, holiness, and redemption.*

*Therefore, as it is written: "Let him who boasts boast
in the Lord" (1 Corinthians 1:26–31).*

Perhaps you have said, "But it wasn't supposed to
happen like this!" So what? Just because your life didn't
fall neatly into place doesn't mean it cannot be a beautiful
mosaic. Your life can be a divine montage, a God-blessed
hodgepodge of experiences. What a story you will have
when people ask how you ended up where you are! You
can tell them that the divine Mosaic Maker called you.

SHOULD I GET PAID FOR THIS CALL?

6

The English word call *comes from the Latin* vocatio, *from which we also get the word* vocation. *Thus, our call and how we earn a living are not unrelated topics.*

The book *How to Succeed in Business Without Losing Your Faith* opens with a story of Roger. Roger had picked up Ed Dayton at the airport in Denver and was driving his guest to an engagement where Mr. Dayton was to speak that evening.

Roger knew that Mr. Dayton had been an aerospace executive before going to seminary and then going to work full-time for a Christian organization. Roger, a businessman, said, "It must be great to do what you are doing. I wish there was some way I could get out of this rat race and really do something for God."

Roger's comment reflects a sincere desire to serve God with all his life. Yet it also reflects what I believe must be the feeling of a lot of people: that in order to "really do something for God" they would have to leave the world of business, go to seminary, and join the staff of some church or Christian organization.

The truth is, we can serve God well, and follow His will, in the marketplace, in the school, and in the neighborhood. Some of the most effective and meaningful ministry is taking place far beyond the walls of a church building. You can live a missional life at Microsoft, in Best Buy, at the ball field, or in the concert hall.

Perhaps more than ever, the future of the Christian movement depends on laypersons. In this chapter I will stress three critical concerns for the lay Christian: your role at church, your role at work, and even the possibility that God might call you (yes, you) to vocational ministry.

Your church needs you. Badly. Acts 6:2 tells of a time the apostles gathered the first church together for a conference. The church was growing. Needs were expanding. Organization was needed. This was the beginning of the *complexification* of the church.

I imagine that Acts 6 meeting going this way…

James spoke up: "I propose a formula for meeting the needs of the Grecian widows. My proposal is that we elect laypersons to minister to them." Peter responded, "Now don't get carried away, Jim. We apostles are the *real* ministers. We know that our members are ministered to only if *we* do the ministry. So instead of working 10 hours a day, we'll work 12!"

One of the church members chimed in and agreed. "That's right. The rest of us are supposed to pray and pay, but *you guys* are the *ministers*."

Then one of the older members of the church stood. Because it was so unlike him to say anything in public, everyone quieted while he spoke. "When I joined this group some time ago," he said, "there were only a handful of us. We knew each other by name, and all of us could fit into one rather small building.

"But things are different now. We've become a large group. And if we are going to insist that the apostles take care of everyone personally, then we are going to stifle our growth. They can't do everything. "Besides, it seems to me that we are all priests!"

At that, the congregation began to murmur. "No, listen," the older man insisted. "The apostles are not the only ministers here. All believers are ministers. I think James's idea is better than any plan I've heard!"

When the gentleman finished, James said, "All in favor of electing seven men to take care of the Greek widows, please say, 'Amen.'" And the place echoed with a unanimous affirmation that every member of that Jerusalem church was a minister.

There is far too much ministry to be done for us to rely only on paid staff. Of course an increasing involvement by laypersons is going to require a shift in attitude for some of us.

I've tried to imagine what it must have been like the first day Stephen, the new lay minister, brought the food to a widow's door. (We'll call the widow Miss Deborah.)

Each Friday the church's widow ministry team prepared fish dinners and dough cakes and the apostles delivered them to the widows of the church. Miss Deborah looked forward to that because she really enjoyed her weekly visit from Peter the apostle. She answered the knock at the door and was visibly shocked when she opened the door and it wasn't Peter standing there.

"Who are you"? she asked.

Her visitor, smiling and holding a plate of fish from the church, answered, "Good morning, Miss Deborah. My name is Stephen. I'll be delivering your food from the church each Friday."

"Where's Peter?"

"I'm taking Peter's place. You know, our church has grown so much that the church decided to select seven men to help out with things, and I'm one of them."

"Is Peter sick?"

"No, ma'am."

"Is he mad at me?"

"No, ma'am."

"Is Peter getting lazy on me?"

"No, ma'am. As I said, the apostles can't be everywhere, and so our organization is changing, you know, adapting. I'm thrilled to be able to bring your fish and cake."

"Well, I miss Peter," said Miss Deborah. "But I understand. And you seem like an awfully nice man. From now on I will look forward to seeing you, Stephen."

As he turned and walked away, Stephen thanked God for Miss Deborah and for the opportunity to engage in ministry that he loved. And he prayed that the whole congregation would understand the importance of lay ministry.

Effective churches of the twenty-first century will take a page from the first-century church's strategy book and emphasize the mobilization of their members. There are a couple of reasons for that.

First is the possibility of a shortage of clergy. In many churches and countries, there are fewer people going into vocational ministry. (By the way, when I say *vocational ministry*, I simply mean ministry from which one earns a living, or at least a part-time salary.) Some are going into vocational ministry as a second career, and have fewer years to offer to the church. Many who are entering vocational ministry are choosing opportunities outside the local church, preferring counseling, social ministry, chaplaincy, etc., to a position in a local congregation. The results of a shortage of clergy in the future is alarming.

Besides that, even if there were an abundance of "paid ministers," lay ministry simply is the most biblical way to meet people's needs and strengthen the church. Lay ministry is the New Testament model. Ephesians 4:11–13, for example, tells us that the responsibility of those we might now call church staff is "to prepare God's people for works of service, so that the body of Christ may be built up." And in verse 16 of that same chapter we read that the body of Christ will be "built up in love" only when "each part does its work."

The church is obviously not the only option for service; there are countless wonderful service organizations besides the church. A lot of people are being salt and light in their community. The church is not the only avenue through which we can serve.

However, for most followers of Jesus, I believe the church should be the primary avenue of volunteer service. (If the church were all we should be, there might not be a *need* for those other organizations.)

Furthermore, lay ministry is not limited to voluntary service. You serve God through your vocation too.

Work (even secular work) is holy. Do you know where we got the phrase "Protestant work ethic"? One of the fundamental convictions of Martin Luther and others who led the Protestant Reformation was that in God's eyes the work of the pastor, or priest, is in no way superior to that of the farmer, the housekeeper, or the businessperson. Work came to be viewed as obedience to God. Puritans and Quakers brought that work ethic to the New World and wove it into the moral and economic fabric of our nation.

The prioritizing of work, however, goes back farther than the Protestant Reformation. It goes back to the opening pages of the Bible. The first picture we get of God is God at work! When the curtain opened on the drama we call history, the main character was already on stage. What was He doing? He was working. Genesis 2:2 reads: "By the seventh day God had finished the work He had been doing." He'd been busy making the grass to grow, the water to flow, the rooster to crow, the wind to blow, the moon to glow, and the snow to snow. The first time we see God, He is at work.

Then "God took the man and put him in the Garden of Eden to work it," says Genesis 2:15. Work was given at the get-go as a perfect part of God's plan, not as a result of sin. Because God is a worker, and because work was a key element of God's original plan for us, your work is holy.

You serve God through the church, but I don't want you to think you are serving God *only* when you're serving on a committee or teaching a Bible study on Sunday morning. You are serving God *also* through your secular work.

John Beckett is president of a company that produces components for residential heating systems. A few years ago the *ABC Evening News* did a piece that centered on him. Peter Jennings introduced it like this:

It seems that everywhere you turn in America these days, millions of people are searching for greater meaning in their lives. Tonight we're going to concentrate on the growing tendency of business leaders in America to have their personal faith make an impact in their companies. In other words, they are using the Bible as a guide to business.

The news piece went on to describe how Beckett is living out his faith in the workplace. The reporter asked Beckett about his life's purpose, and he answered, "My main mission in life is to know the will of God and to do it." Beckett is living his mission out on Monday through Friday as well as on Sunday.

If you are doing what God created you to do, then you are living out your mission. When you repair that engine, balance those books, start that IV, teach that class, administer that office, or make that sale, you are doing the will of God. From farming to pharmacy. From bookkeeping to beekeeping. From the changing of the guards at Buckingham Palace to the changing of the diapers at *your* palace, your work—yes, even your *secular* work—is holy, if that is what God created you to do.

Find your vocational calling. (Find how God wants you to earn a living.)

Work takes up so many of our waking hours that our jobs come to define us and give us our identities. We become what we do. Calling reverses such thinking. A sense of calling should precede a choice of job and career, and the main way to discover calling is along the line of what we are each

*created and gifted to be. Instead of "You are what you do,"
calling says, "Do what you are."*—Os Guinness, *The Call*

Life is too short for you and me to work merely for a pay-
check. It might be that the reason you are holding this book
is that God is prompting you to step out in faith and find
your vocational calling. There are career counselors out
there who can help you. Or maybe you already know, deep
in your heart, what you ought to be doing from 9:00 to 5:00.
What remains now is for you to trust God enough to follow a
call not so different from Abraham's—to leave your security
for a life God will reveal to you little by little.

If you are considering new employment, I highly recommend the book by Richard N. Bolles, *What Color Is Your
Parachute?* Bolles embraces the concept of a divine call
when it comes to one's vocation, and the epilogue, "How
to Find Your Mission in Life," is worth the price of the book.
Bolles writes, concerning God's vocational calling, that your
mission is

a) *to exercise that talent which you particularly came to
earth to use—your greatest gift, which you most delight
to use,*
b) *in the place(s) or setting(s) which God has caused to
appeal to you the most,*
c) *and for those purposes which God most needs to have
done in the world.*

Here is a quick note to those who might be reading this
book because you are between jobs and seeking God's will
for employment. Bolles writes that unemployment provides

us with a chance "to marry our work and our religious beliefs together, to talk about calling, and vocation, and mission in life—to think out why we are here, and what plans God has for us. That's why a period of unemployment can absolutely change our life."

Can a vocational calling change? I think so. Some believe that a calling to vocational ministry is an irreversible, lifetime call. I'm not so sure about that. If God can lead a dedicated Christian banker into a position of administrator for a non-profit corporation, can He not also lead a youth pastor into a role as a high school counselor? If passion has so much to do with our call, then what if our passion changes? What if we acquire new skills that God could use in a different (secular) role? I don't think a person should abandon a vocational call casually. But neither would I rule out a potential, God-pleasing change.

Maybe that's a mystery for both of us to ponder.

Consider vocational ministry. In our attempts to emphasize that every Christian is a minister, we might have unintentionally dissuaded some folks from entering vocational ministry. I hope that's not the case, for I enthusiastically encourage people to consider a call to vocational ministry, no matter where they are in life. I do that for two reasons. One, I think it is absolutely a wonderful life! Two, I love the church and am concerned that the church have good staff leadership.

Over the last few years Bon Air Baptist Church has called several senior staff members from within our congregation. For example...

Our present student minister came to us out of the mulch industry.

Our present site pastor (pastor of our second campus) came to us from the greenhouse industry.

Our present associate pastor for member mobilization came to us out of retirement from public school teaching.

They all have brought to us a known commitment to our church, a deep passion for what they are doing, fantastic God-given skills, the probability that they are going to have a long tenure with us, and an understanding of our culture. Our staff and our church are enriched by them. They relate to regular folks wonderfully. In short, they are outstanding ministers.

One of the most effective ministries our church has is NorthStar Community, a Christ-centered recovery ministry. NorthStar has been recognized as one of the ten leading church-based recovery ministries in the nation. That amazing ministry is staffed by three nonordained nonseminarians, none of whom has previous experience on a church staff. One was a full-time housewife, and the others left secular careers. **God is transforming lives through all the above staff members, though they would never have been even considered by some congregational search committees.**

It was natural for our church to bring these folks on staff. Our church's emphasis on spiritual gifts as a basis for ministry, and our intentional efforts to mobilize our members, make calling staff members from out of the congregation seem natural.

Our church does not ignore the importance of experience, and experience on other church staffs still is valued by our search teams. Yet we believe the experience that all of these new staff members have gotten as dedicated volunteers *in our church* is valuable as well.

We also value theological education at our church, and seminary degrees are still preferable for us when it comes to paid staff. Yet there is a lot to be said for church-based ministerial training. (Many believe that within the next several decades theological education will return to the church.) So we have instituted a church-based plan whereby these staff members are getting the equipping we believe they need. Supervised reading, mentoring by experienced staff members with theological/ministerial degrees, tailor-made seminars, and individualized distance learning classes from highly esteemed seminaries provide helpful avenues by which we fashion programs, based on the individual and his or her position on the staff.

Please don't misunderstand; I do recognize the importance of formal theological education. Our son, Landon, says at this point that he believes God is leading him toward vocational youth ministry, and I highly recommend that Landon get a good theological/ministerial education. Nothing takes the place of the intensive academic discipline that a seminary or Bible school offers. The gaining of knowledge is important, and training in critical thinking is vital.

However, I recognize the value of a heart that is devoted to Christian ministry, and the worth of experience and personal study. All things being equal, a formal theological education is a great advantage in ministry. Yet if I have to choose between a well-educated ministry "professional" and someone who has no formal training yet loves Jesus and loves people and has the passion and gifts to equip fellow believers for doing ministry…I'll take the latter any day.

Apparently a lot of people agree with me, for a lot of churches nowadays are calling their ministerial staff from within the congregation. Some think it's a fad; I tend to believe it is a movement of God's Spirit—one of the indications of a church in transition. Is anyone reading this who has had some sense that God might be leading you to a role on the staff of a local church or some other vocational ministry? Are you willing to consider that possibility?

There is a lot of effective, intentional, missional living by people who don't draw paychecks from Christian organizations. Just don't rule out the possibility that God is calling you to a ministry vocation.

Why not check your COMPASS and see where it points? It might indicate that you already are right where you ought to be, doing exactly what God created you to do. On the other hand, you might be pointed toward a new secular vocation, a new volunteer ministry, or even a role on the paid staff of a local church.

CALL FOLLOWING REQUIRES CHARACTER

7

For the adventurous journey you certainly need a COMPASS. Yet who you are is more important than all the tools in your backpack.

A call from the Creator of the universe demands the best we have. And our best is found not primarily in what we do, but in who we are when no one is looking—our character.

No matter how well-educated or well-connected we are. No matter how impressive our résumés or how stylish our wardrobes. No matter how gracious, gregarious, gutsy, or "go-getting" we are. If we don't have a strong character, we will fall short of our calling. In this chapter we will explore some of the fundamental distinctives about the character of an effective, missional Christ follower.

SERVANT SPIRIT

Os Guinness said in *The Call,* "God normally calls us along the line of our giftedness, but the purpose of giftedness is stewardship and service, not selfishness." Jesus taught that principle the night He washed the disciples' feet. Read about it in John 13:1–14.

There were a lot of elephants in the upper room that night; a lot of issues were going unmentioned. The first issue was the incessant competition between the disciples over who was top dog. Luke wrote in his account of this event that even during the Last Supper a dispute arose among them as to which of them was considered to be greatest.

Second was the fact that the disciples had spent virtually every moment together for months and months and months. Don't you imagine, for example, they had gotten on each other's nerves? Don't you imagine that a lot of those guys still resented the fact that Matthew used to be a tax collector? Don't you imagine they had had all they could take of Peter's propensity for popping off?

Third was the dirty feet. Everybody there had on sandals, which were nothing more than soles with a few straps, and they all had walked through dust and mud and who knows what else in the days before rest areas. In many social settings a servant would have the responsibility to wash their feet, but none of them was going to do such a menial task, especially given their history of competing for the title of "greatest." So they just ignored the mud-caked feet at the end of all the legs in the room.

Fourth was the fact that Judas was going to betray Jesus and Jesus knew it. The others had to suspect something.

Then, with one simple act, Jesus addressed every elephant in the room. He washed all those dirty feet. Including the feet of Judas.

John 13:3, 4, 5 says: *"Jesus knew that the Father had put all things under his power, and that he had come from God and was returning to God,* **so** *he got up...and...began to wash his disciples' feet."*

That little word *so* is far more important than its two lowercase letters would indicate. Listen to its impact: Jesus was secure in who He was, **so** (therefore, thus, thereupon, hence, consequently, ergo) He was able to serve His disciples. Because Jesus understood His identity and His call, He could humble Himself.

Somewhere I read this Oriental proverb: "The fuller the ear is of rice grain, the lower it bends." Jesus, fully aware of and comfortable with His identity, was able to bend low enough to wash those dirty feet.

I believe some of us find it hard to be servants because of our insecurities and feelings of inferiority. If we feel inadequate, then we have a constant need to prove ourselves, to try to convince ourselves and others that we are worthy of their respect. We do things that make ourselves look good in order to cover up for what we feel are shortcomings. To do something seemingly demeaning to ourselves would be the last thing we'd consider. Yet when we are secure and comfortable with who we are then (1) life is not one big competition, so we aren't trying to prove our value by "beating" each other; and (2) we don't feel we have to be the center of attention, so taking a submissive role is not threatening. Therefore, if we are secure and comfortable with who we are in Christ, then we can serve without hesitation.

All of us can feel secure and confident in who we are. We are God's treasures, His creation, His handiwork. In Jeremiah 1:5, God tells us He formed us, molded and shaped us, in the womb. If babies came with designer labels, every label would read: *Designed by the Creator of the Universe.*

Moreover, followers of Jesus are children of the King! We are forgiven, free, temples of God's Spirit, and bound for heaven.

If we will only remember who we are, then acts of service will come much easier.

Servanthood does not come naturally for some of us. A few years ago I took a spiritual gifts inventory. I was sobered (but not surprised) by the fact that I did not score very high in the category of service. I'm ashamed to admit that servanthood is not my strong suit. Of course, I can't just dismiss that and say, "Well, that's not my gift." That would be a cop-out. I want to be more servantlike, so this section is certainly as much for me as for any reader.

So how can we prime the servant pump? Two suggestions:

One, let's act humbly when no one is looking. Nobody saw Jesus with the towel except His disciples. This was not a performance for the crowd. This was a genuinely humble act, behind closed doors. Jesus warned us, *"Be careful not to do your 'acts of righteousness' before men, to be seen by them"* (Matthew 6:1).

Service is hard for us, and "secret" service is doubly difficult. Richard Foster wrote in *Celebration of Discipline,* "The flesh whines against service, but screams against hidden service. It strains and pulls for honor and recognition." By nature we want people to notice our acts of goodness. By doing things that no one will celebrate, or even know about, we can become a little more like Jesus. Through intentionally anonymous acts—through doing things and making sure nobody knows about them—perhaps we can break the hold that our natural desire for accolades has on us.

Two, let's wash the feet of our Judases. Jesus washed Judas's feet. I think I would have slapped him, scalped him, or at least skipped him. But Jesus washed his feet!

I walked out of a rather contentious meeting over 20 years ago alongside a man who had squared off against two men in a church power struggle. The man beside me was accustomed to having things go his way, but they hadn't gone his way that night. He growled, loud enough for me to hear, "I'm tired of getting run over by people smaller than I am."

Judas was infinitely "smaller" than Jesus, and was about to "run over Him." Yet Jesus washed his feet.

Jesus told us, *"You have heard that it was said, 'Love your neighbor and hate your enemy.' But I tell you: Love your enemies"* (Matthew 5:43–44). The verb there is an active verb. It is more than tolerating our personal Judases. It is more than a refraining from slapping, scalping, or skipping them. It is an active and intentional expression of love toward those who don't love us back.

That is risky. We are perhaps never more vulnerable than when we love those who would just as soon betray us as look at us. (And you will encounter such people as you follow your call.) We are perhaps never more vulnerable than when we love those who would turn on us if there were something in it for them. The ultimate act of service, perhaps, is to somehow perform an act of service for our Judas.

How would it be if you were to say a word of encouragement to someone who does not support your vision, but who has done a really fine job at something? How would it be if, without jeopardizing the organization or sacrificing your convictions, you were to yield to someone who always seems to oppose you? **I can't think of**

anything that would strengthen our character, and make service more natural, than to choose love for those who don't love us in return.

CLEAN LIVING

It is critical that you and I maintain pure lifestyles that do not in any way discredit the church, for the greater our involvement in God's kingdom, the greater the negative impact of our failures.

One Sunday morning many years ago my brother-in-law Keith was sitting in the balcony with a fellow teenager during the worship service. His mother was in the choir loft. Keith and his friend had a box of BBs. The floor of the balcony was hardwood, and the balcony has tiers. These two teenage boys were sitting on an upper level. You know where this story is going, don't you?

The pastor was preaching when those boys dropped that box of BBs onto the wooden floor of the balcony. The BBs fell and rolled and fell and rolled and fell and rolled on that unforgiving floor, echoing throughout the church until they reached the rail and finally fell silent. I'm quite certain that no one remembers what happened in that service after the bouncing BBs.

Other mistakes probably occurred in that same service but were not as noticeable. Perhaps a child on the bottom floor dropped a doll onto the carpet and hardly anyone knew. Maybe a man nodded off to sleep, and unless someone saw his wife punch him in the ribs no one else knew. But two teenagers in the balcony with BBs and a wooden floor—their mistake impacted a lot of folks! The boys' mistake wasn't worse than others, but their profile was higher, and the impact of their misdeed was farther reaching.

When a Christian with a high profile fails morally, the negative impact on his or her corner of the world is significant. If you are following a call, people know it, and that gives you the kind of profile that makes the BBs you drop more disruptive than those dropped by others. Call it a double standard if you like, but that's the way it is.

Self-control is essential to clean living. Clean, holy living is largely a product of self-control, and there are many references to self-control in the Bible. There are no secrets, no shortcuts that can substitute for good, old-fashioned self-control—the strength of character to draw a line in the sand and say, "I will not cross this line because to do so is wrong."

But self-control is more than merely gritting our teeth and denying ourselves pleasure. The ability to say no comes best from what author Stephen Covey called a deep, burning yes.

Russ Rainer is a former member of the US Olympic wrestling team. I asked him to tell me what drives an Olympic athlete to sacrifice free time, relationships, and finances in order to pursue a medal. Russ answered, "You hear a voice deep inside even during times of frustration, pain, and loss. The voice is always telling you not to give up the vision and to fight on." That voice of which Russ spoke is that deep, burning yes—the goal, the prize, that is worth all the self-denial along the way.

What does that have to do with us? Our sense of call—the recognition that the Creator of the universe laid His hand on us and directed us into particular service opportunities —ought to be our deep, burning yes. Passion for our calls empowers us to say no to those things that could shatter our lives and ministries, and bring shame upon the family of God.

Clean living requires that we avoid tempting, questionable situations. Jesus Himself, in the Model Prayer, taught us to pray that God would deliver us from temptation. Hear also Proverbs 6:27–28 (KJV): *"Can a man take fire in his bosom, and his clothes not be burned? Can one go upon hot coals, and his feet not be burned?"*

Notice in Titus 2 that Paul instructed Titus to teach the older women himself. However, he told Titus to let the *older* women teach the *younger* women. Why would Paul make such a distinction between Titus's interactions with older and younger women? It might have been that Paul wanted to keep Titus away from tempting situations, or from situations in which his time spent with the young women might have been perceived wrongly. Those of us who have responded to the divine call must avoid tempting situations. We must also avoid appearances of wrongdoing, for even rumors can threaten our credibility.

Countless ministers—both vocational and volunteer—have blown great opportunities and disgraced the family of faith because of sinful choices. Almost never did they set out to mess things up. Little by little, however, they drifted into the kinds of indiscretions that shatter lives. Counseling sessions got too personal. Two people working together on a spiritual project spent so much time together that their relationship became terribly unspiritual. People got careless and messed up.

The legend is told of a man standing on a high cliff overlooking the river below. He saw in the distance a carcass floating down the river. As it came closer he could see that it was a sheep's carcass, and on top of that carcass sat an eagle, having dinner. (A dinner cruise, I guess you could call it.) Up ahead there was a high and treacherous waterfall.

As the eagle ate, the onlooker from the cliff imagined that the eagle was aware of the waterfall; yet the eagle was in no hurry. The eagle's mighty wings would carry him from danger in due time. So he ate until his instincts told him that it was time to fly.

The eagle finally spread those majestic pinions and prepared to take flight. He called on his great strength to propel him beyond the danger of the approaching cascade. He flapped his wings...but nothing happened. He flapped them again...but could not fly away. His claws had become entangled in the wool of that carcass, and he couldn't free himself. He flapped and flapped...until he, still entangled in the wool, went over the waterfall to his death.

A lot of good folks have gotten entangled in things about which they knew better...and plunged over the waterfall. They thought that, in due time, they would abandon their "feast." When it came time to fly, however, they found it was too late.

There are various potential entanglements. I am going to focus here on sexual offenses, and I choose to do that for three reasons: (1) sexual misbehavior is far too common, even among Christians; (2) sexual sin is particularly scandalous and does great damage to the family of God; and (3) our sexual natures exist at a deep emotional place in us; if the enemy can hurt us there, he can hurt us deeply.

1. Decide now on the situations you will intentionally avoid. For example...

- Don't work alone after hours with someone of the opposite sex, especially if one or both of you are married.
- Do everything within your power to avoid traveling on business trips with someone of the opposite sex.

I even suggest being very careful about frequent business meals with only one other person of the opposite sex, if one or both of you are married. I realize that business lunches between members of the opposite sex are part of American business culture, and that many of you couldn't do your work without them. However, my hunch is that more than a few inappropriate relationships have been planted over coffee and dessert. Just be careful to keep it professional. When it is possible, the better part of wisdom probably is to have a third person join you.

2. Be wary of discussions about emotional, intimate, personal issues (particularly marital problems) with people of the opposite sex. If you are perceived as a spiritual person, then people will drop their guard with you. Even people of the opposite sex will discuss intimate details of their lives with you. Those discussions usually begin with innocent motives, yet those conversations take you to a level of emotional connectedness that is risky. If you are a vocational minister, talking about those things is sometimes necessary in a counseling setting, but remaining "professional" is critical. If you are not a vocational minister, I can think of no situation in which you should engage in a deep conversation with someone of the opposite sex about emotional, intimate, personal issues. Those conversations simply take two people to an emotionally volatile depth, and should take place between people of the same gender.

3. If you are married, talk about your boundaries with your spouse. No matter how good our marriages or how strong our convictions, we all are vulnerable. Agree together and beforehand on the lines that you will draw. Will you call each other before you go to lunch with persons of the opposite sex? Will you take unaccompanied trips with persons of the opposite sex? Will you carry on emotionally involved conversations with the opposite sex? Those are questions you and your spouse need to answer together before you face those situations and have to make a decision on the spot.

4. Be wary of affairs of the heart. Every time I speak publicly about emotional affairs it seems to strike a chord. Many are the people who began to flirt innocently with someone in the office, began to share things on a level that is way too deep emotionally, and began to imagine what it would be like to be alone with that person. They started dabbing on a little extra cologne when they knew they were going to see that certain person. They never intended to have an affair, but one day an opportunity presented itself and, entangled in each other's arms, they went over the waterfall. At the bottom awaited broken promises, broken hearts, and broken homes.

If you find yourself entertaining thoughts about someone besides your spouse, you'd better fly now, before you get entangled! The waterfall is not far ahead.

5. If you are married, nurture your marriage. The best insurance against infidelity is a strong, loving marriage. Every day millions of men and women work together in the marketplace and maintain professional, appropriate relationships. Every day thousands of counseling situations occur without even the hint of anything inappropriate. I don't want to leave the impression that we should be paranoid about what our spouses are doing during the day. However, every day somebody somewhere crosses a line and wrecks a life.

Even people carrying a COMPASS can wander off the trail if they aren't vigilant. So let's be careful. Not paranoid, or prudish, but prudent.

WILLINGNESS TO STAND WITH FEET IN TWO DIFFERENT BOATS

Lyle Schaller wrote a book about the church in America and its future. He titled it, *Discontinuity and Hope.* I think that title sums up the future of the church in America, and in the rest of the world, for that matter. I have hope for the church's future. That hope, however, comes with the understanding that, in Yogi Berra's words, "The future ain't what it used to be."

We live in a period of big-time transition. We have entered what has been appropriately labeled a TEOTWAWKI culture—The End of the World as We Know It. In *The Church on the Other Side,* Brian McLaren makes a poignant statement: "If you have a new world, you need a new church. You have a new world." Well, our world certainly is changing, and those changes demand increasingly creative approaches to ministry. Our present time of transition—what some are calling a new reformation—makes for significant instability.

The way we've done church for the last several decades seems to be increasingly less effective. Churches are plateauing, declining, and even closing all across the country. The arrival of postmodernity has us all wondering what the future church is going to look like. It is a time of transition; we are between eras. As a church leader, I often feel like I am standing on a lake with one foot in one boat and the other foot in another boat. It's a bit wobbly. Unsteady. Uncertain.

This "in-between" time is not only uncomfortable; it is volatile. Well known is the conflict between those who want to hang onto the past, those who want to jettison the past, and those who aren't sure *what* they want.

Ministry in this transitional time is not for cowards. Handling change requires the best leadership we can muster. Change is difficult, and should not be embraced capriciously; but change is necessary, and should not be resisted stubbornly. We must hold in tension those two truths. If we either initiate change without sensitivity to tradition, or oppose change for the mere sake of tradition, we will jeopardize the health of the organization in question.

Change can be traumatic for humans, but the absence of change can be worse. Careless change can ravage an organization, but without change the organization will atrophy. To strike the balance requires discernment and courage. **Navigating the transition that the church in North America is experiencing requires the ability to say no to some changes, when revolutionaries would traumatize the organization. It also requires the willingness to revise**

the course when staunch traditionalists would let the organization die a slow and agonizing, suffocating death.

So far, the church I serve as pastor is striking the balance between traditionalism and tumultuous change. That is a testimony to our members' flexibility and missional spirit. They really are an exceptionally flexible, patient, and positive bunch of folks. But I have to tell you, sometimes striking that balance between traditionalism and tumultuous change feels like standing on the lake with feet in two boats!

You have been chosen by God to live in this era of transition. To follow a call and help others with their calls during this in-between period is no small task. You will feel the pull on one side from those who want to keep things as they are. You will feel the pull on the other side from those who want to change everything yesterday. Ministry in this period of transition is not easy; yet it is not impossible. In many ways it is even exhilarating. You *can* keep your balance with feet in two boats.

A GROWING, INTIMATE
RELATIONSHIP WITH GOD

Discerning the voice of God requires our remaining near enough to God that we can hear Him whisper. The character necessary to follow that call requires a close relationship with our Father as well.

Exit Interviews, by William D. Hendricks, is a book that explores the stories of multitudes who have left the church—those who have either stormed out angrily or just drifted out apathetically. William Hendricks, the author, asked people, "Why did you leave?"

One of the most telling revelations is what the book calls

"the red herring of busyness." A red herring is something meant to distract. It comes from the idea of dragging a red herring (fish) across the road with the hope that its scent would throw one's pursuer offtrack. According to Hendricks's research, a number of people who have left the church got disgusted with the fact that church folks try to substitute busyness for spirituality. "A number of interviewees pointed out that heavy involvement in programs and church or ministry-related activities is neither a sign of spirituality nor a means toward it....One could be busy serving the Lord, yet starving inside due to a lack of intimacy with God." Surely they weren't talking about your church or my church!

The attempt to substitute busyness for an intimate relationship with God is akin to the attempt of people long ago to substitute calves and firstborns for that relationship:

> *"With what shall I come before the LORD and bow down before the exalted God? Shall I come before him with burnt offerings, with calves a year old? Will the LORD be pleased with thousands of rams, with ten thousand rivers of oil? Shall I offer my firstborn for my transgression, the fruit of my body for the sin of my soul? He has showed you, O man, what is good. And what does the LORD require of you? To act justly and to love mercy and to walk humbly with your God" (Micah 6:6–8).*

Paul Overstreet must have had this text in mind when he wrote the song that he sang with Tanya Tucker. One stanza of that song says:

> *"How much do I owe you? said the man to his Lord....*
> *Shall I build a temple, shall I make a sacrifice?""*

And the answer comes back:

> *"I won't take less than your love, sweet love....All*
> *the treasures of the world would never be enough,*
> *and I won't take less than your love."*

God isn't looking for temples and sacrifice. Nor is He looking for busyness. He is looking for relationship. It was for that purpose that we were created. God wants nothing less. Activity is no substitute, no matter how admirable the activity.

I have long loved the story of a young woman and her father who took long walks together each morning. They would talk about life and their problems and their delights. It was the father's great joy to spend time in such a close relationship with his daughter.

Then, as Christmas approached one year, the young woman decided to sew an article of clothing for her father. It was a big project that took a great deal of her time. So she suspended her morning walks with her dad in order to make him a gift.

On Christmas Day she presented her gift to her dad, proud of the fact that she had made it herself. He loved his gift, and was very gracious. But soon he had to express his feelings. With kindness in his heart and voice he said, "Sweetheart, next year skip the gift and just walk with me."

"Don't choose the work of the Lord over the Lord of the work." I love that phrase! I learned it from Otis Williams, supervisor of a youth revival team I was on back in 1979. He knew how busy we would be, traveling all over Alabama to do two youth revivals per week. And he rightfully suggested that busyness in the Lord's work is not the same as nurturing our relationship with the Lord.

THE PRACTICE OF SPIRITUAL DISCIPLINES

Do you always test your antifreeze before winter? It's a good idea to test your antifreeze to see if it is able to protect your car in the really cold weather. You stick a tester into the antifreeze and it will say the antifreeze is good to 30 degrees below zero, or 10 below, or maybe "Your car is protected only if you live in Miami." During pleasant weather, just about any old antifreeze will do. Weak antifreeze, however, will not protect you when it gets extremely cold. You will need really good antifreeze when the blizzard hits.

At what point on the scale would your faith, or spirituality, give out? Down to what point would it be effective in sustaining you, in keeping you going?

Any old religion is sufficient when things are sunny. A little religion is fine, if things are going well. But when the blizzard sets in and the bottom falls out (and be sure that it will), then you need something substantial. When deep cries out to deep, shallow religion won't cut it. (My inspiration for this section came from *Riverside Sermons*, by Harry Emerson Fosdick).

When Keri and I were newly married I was not committed to the daily discipline of prayer and Bible study. I didn't exactly practice what I preached in that department. But I can't tell you how many times I'd walk through our house or apartment and find Keri alone, having her daily quiet time with God. Quietly, without drawing any attention to it, since her college days she has spent a long time every morning alone with God. For all those years, with her Bible in her lap and her journal on the couch beside her, she has entered daily what Oswald Chambers called "the workshop."

When we moved to Nigeria as missionaries, those first few weeks were tough. Electricity and water were all too rare in that house in the ancient city of Oyo where we studied the Yoruba language. Our three-year-old daughter contracted malaria in record time. A heat rash transformed our ten-month-old into a living, breathing, scratching reminder of the torture to which we were subjecting our poor, innocent children. Language study was about as much fun as, well, language study. These trials, together with the newness of the culture, nearly propelled me past culture shock to culture electrocution.

For a month I prayed for a rare tropical disease. I wasn't suicidal; I was merely searching for an honorable way to exit. I didn't want to die; I just wanted to get sick enough to get sent home and save face.

After a few months I broke through "the wall," and we all ended up *loving* Nigeria. Life and ministry there were very rewarding. Years later, when we were unable to return to Nigeria because of my parents' ill health, that was painful and discouraging. But initially being in Nigeria was tough, and I didn't do so well.

Keri, on the other hand, was much stronger than I was during those early, trying days. Far more disciplined. Much more at peace. I recall realizing at least one reason why that was true. I was terribly inconsistent in my devotional life, but I happened to be reading the Bible one morning when I suddenly understood why Keri was coping far better than I was; it was because of her daily discipline of meeting with God. I can remember the feel of the cement floor under my feet and the weight in my heart as I said to Keri, "You are stronger than I am because your relationship with God is stronger than mine." It was from that time that I began my personal daily practice of prayer and Bible study.

When deep cried out to deep, I had nothing to draw from. Keri did. Keri had a depth of spirituality that I didn't have. When deep cried out to deep, my wife had a strength that I had only preached about. She had cultivated a deep relationship with God through the practice of spiritual disciplines.

Phillips Brooks wrote:

> Some day, in the years to come, you will be wrestling with the great temptation, or trembling under the great sorrow of your life. But the real struggle is here, now....Now it is being decided whether, in the day of your supreme sorrow or temptation, you shall miserably fail or gloriously conquer. Character cannot be made except by a steady, long continued process.

And that steady, long-continued process involves what we call spiritual disciplines. I believe prayer, fasting, and Bible study are the staples of the spiritual disciplines. Following are some of the other spiritual disciplines that are paramount for those who are following a call. I find these of particular importance to call followers, and yet particularly difficult for call followers to practice.

Public Worship. We all need experiences of genuine worship. If you are on staff at a church, or have a ministry role that demands your attention and energy on Sundays, you will be tempted to see the worship service as "work." If you can't get yourself in the mind-set for genuine worship on Sundays, then you'd better find some means of filling that void, for we all need genuine experiences of corporate worship.

Fellowship. One of the most difficult aspects of ministry is loneliness. If you are a layperson and seriously committed to your calling, you will find that you are in a small fraternity. If you are a vocational minister, it will be hard to find close relationships. Most other ministers are too busy in their own worlds to have time for relationships; and nonministers don't quite know how to treat you. You will have to be intentional about establishing and nurturing close friendships.

Solitude. Being silent and alone opens the channel through which God often comes to visit with us. The strength you draw from those visits will carry you through a lot of difficulties. Solitude is hard to come by for busy call followers, but without it we draw from a shallow pool of spiritual strength.

When we lived in Oyo, Nigeria, water was scarce, particularly during the dry season. We had a little cistern that held water, and the water in that little cistern was shared by two families (including five small children). We rationed the water and used the same bucket of water two or three times.

I cannot describe to you the stress we experienced over the short supply of water. We'd pray for rain and literally run outside like expectant children at the slightest rumble in the distant sky. I'd chase trucks carrying water begging them to come and fill our little cistern. During dry spells, the little cistern was insufficient, and we didn't have an ample supply of water.

But when we moved to Ogbomosho after language study, we had a huge cistern. Into that cistern flowed water both from the city and from the rainfall. It was deep and big and it supplied our needs even in dry season.

I encourage you to prepare for the inevitable crisis by engaging in the spiritual disciplines. Spiritual disciplines build up a deep reservoir of strength, so that when the dry season comes—the season when there are questions without answers and grief without consolation—when deep cries out to deep, the cistern will sustain you.

Courage. Courage is...wait...on second thought...I think courage deserves a chapter of its own.

COURAGE 8

Some important feats have been accomplished by people who were not particularly skilled, charismatic, or well educated. I can think of nothing of consequence, however, that ever has come about without a good amount of courage.

I don't like high places. I'm downright afraid of them. Yet I'm fascinated by those who are not frightened of heights. A psychology student could write a paper on my neurotic fear-yet-fascination with high things and people who jump off them.

When we were in Florida on a family vacation a few years ago, we went to an amusement park. At the entrance to the park is the bungee jump. You know the bungee jump; that is where seemingly intelligent people place their lives in the hands of a barefooted guy with bleached blond hair, a ponytail, and piercings on several observable body parts and who knows where else. They allow this man to attach a large rubber band to the harness they are wearing and, for reasons which I cannot imagine, throw themselves off a perfectly good platform.

There were bleachers in front of the bungee jump so that people who know better can watch those who *don't* know better jump off a high place. I sat down with my kids on the bleachers. A man and his son climbed the stairs to the platform. The dad was 40ish. The son was 14 or so. The dad went first. He walked somewhat gingerly to the edge of the platform. The mom and sister were sitting near us on the bleachers cheering. "Jump, honey!" yelled his wife (which made me wonder about their relationship).

For a few tense moments we wondered if the poor guy would go through with it. But then he took a deep breath and jumped right off. He bounced like a yo-yo for a few moments, then was lowered to the ground.

His son was next. The man up top hooked the son up to the rubber cord. And the young man, whose name, we overheard, was Adam, inched his way up to the edge of the platform.

He looked over the brink and shook his head. His dad called out, "Jump, Adam! *I* did it! Jump!"

"Jump, Adam!" yelled his little sister. But Adam didn't jump. He just stood there. Finally Adam turned around, and, in front of all those people, walked away. He walked past two others who were waiting to take the plunge. He crept back down the stairs, obviously embarrassed. He couldn't do it. Others had jumped. His dad had jumped. But Adam couldn't do it.

REQUIREMENT: COURAGE

Your COMPASS often is going to point toward ominous territory. The signs will read, *Danger Ahead* or *Proceed at Your Own Risk.* When you stand at the foot of those flashing warning signs it will be decided whether you will boldly follow God's call or ease back into a more comfortable, yet far less effective and far less satisfying way of life.

Doing something you believe God has led you to do is often a bit scary. You might be frightened of criticism or failure. Maybe the thought of public speaking, or confrontation, or of making tough decisions scares you. Perhaps the thought of living in the proverbial fishbowl makes you shake in your proverbial boots. It might be that the idea of doing church in a postmodern culture gives you hives. (If it doesn't, it *should.*) **Deciding to follow a divine call can be daunting. It's a bit like standing on the edge of a bungee platform.**

If there is one thing required of the missional life, it is **courage**. Because courage is so central in the willingness to follow God's call, and to keep following God's call, I've given courage its own chapter.

Wanda Lee, executive director of Woman's Missionary Union, knows how important courage is. She shares in her book, *Live the Call*:

> One day I was visiting with a leader of a large organization, and we shared concerns that we both had about leadership. He asked if he could pray for me, and if so, what would I like for him to pray for specifically. I was humbled by his request and simply asked him to pray that I might have wisdom when facing times of decision making. He paused

for a moment and then asked if he could expand that prayer on my behalf. He said he learned that all the wisdom in the world would not help him unless he had the courage to act on it once he received it. Since that day I have altered my prayer as well. I ask God for His wisdom, but I also ask Him to give me the courage to act when the time is right.

COURAGE AND GOD-GIVEN DREAMS

Do you remember the parable of the talents (found in Matthew 25:14-28)? The talents Jesus spoke of were not what we usually mean by talents. A talent was a very large amount of money. Jesus told the story of a wealthy man who distributed his money among his servants. He gave to one servant five talents, to another two, and to another one, and then he left the country.

Upon his return, he called his servants in to see what they had done with the talents. The first one reported, "Sir, while you were gone, I invested your five talents, and they doubled in value! Here are your ten talents." The second did the same and earned two more talents. The master was thrilled with what his servants had done.

Then the third servant came in. He reported, "Sir, you are going to be proud of me. You gave me one talent, and I am delighted to report that I still have that one talent. You'll notice it's still kind of dirty. That's because I'm so smart I buried it until you returned."

The master was *not* proud. He was angry. "You have been lazy and foolish," stormed the master.

Now, let me ask you a question: What are you doing with your talents? I'm not talking now about money or ability; I'm talking about dreams. What about those unique, God-given dreams that you have? Dreams for your vocation. Dreams for your church. Dreams for that ministry that you lead. Dreams for the organization you serve. Dreams for your life. Are you fulfilling your dreams and potential?

I imagine that some of you reading this book have dreams...good dreams...dreams that you are afraid of pursuing. The pursuit of dreams requires courage. (There was a popular T-shirt a couple of years ago with the words *You can't steal second with your foot on first.*) I don't want to suggest irresponsible, rash, impulsive decisions. And I recognize that there is a fine line between courage and craziness. Nevertheless, I challenge you to courageously pursue your good dreams. Don't turn around and walk down from your bungee platform. Jump!

Remember: One of the elements of God's call to specific tasks is a passion for that task. *"For it is God who works in you to will and to act according to his good purpose"* (Philippians 2:13). Your dream just might be your call! **Check out your dream by your COMPASS, and if you confirm that yours is a God-given dream, then follow it courageously.** It is not unlikely that what you, as a Christ follower, dream of doing is indeed what God wants you to do. Moreover, it would be downright sinful to bury a dream that God has entrusted to you.

LESSON FROM AN INTRUDER

It was a Friday night in the fall of 1981. I was house-sitting for friends in Caracas, Venezuela. They were to be gone for a week and they asked me to stay there and watch the house and their dog. They explained that they always left the sliding glass door slightly ajar so that the dog could come and go.

That Friday night I woke up to sirens, voices, and searchlights. I watched through the window as the police obviously searched for someone...and never found him. They left alone. The one for whom the police were looking was still at large.

The very next night I was awakened again in the middle of the night. The dog was in the next room, growling. I'd not heard the dog growl like that before. He sounded half mad and half scared. I got up to see what it was. I walked into the family room and through the kitchen door I saw the dog in the kitchen. He was looking up, about eye level, into a part of the kitchen beyond my view. I could not see what the dog was looking at, but the dog and I were obviously not alone.

I thought back to the previous night when the police left without finding who they were looking for. I deduced that the object of the unsuccessful manhunt was now in the house with me. I looked over at the sliding glass door standing slightly open, and I knew that was how he entered.

My first thought was to find something to defend myself. I spied two decorative spears on the wall and thought of grabbing one. Then I thought, "No, he'll take that away from me and kill me with it."

Then I decided to try to talk to him. I had been there for only a few weeks, and my Spanish was terrible. In Spanish I said something like this: "Me leave. You stay. Me go out door. Never say nothing. Take house. Take dog. Me leaving."

I got no response.

And then I decided to stand my ground. I thought, "At

least I'll die a hero." So I got ready. I took several deep breaths, and psyched myself up. And I charged toward the kitchen.

I jumped around the corner with a yell and turned mid-air in the direction which the dog was facing.

Our eyes met immediately.

For some reason the intruder was on top of the sink. That's where the dog had been facing and growling. But when I bounded into the kitchen, I scared the prowler so badly he panicked. He jumped at the window and the window was closed. Boom! He fell from the window and hit the ground on the run. He ran past me and out the open sliding glass door with the dog right behind him.

I was still scared, long after he was gone. I tried to laugh, for it was comical to see the intruder…a stray cat…flying out the door with the dog on his tail.

I faced the situation not knowing what was awaiting me, and it turned out not to be as bad as I had feared. There is a lesson in that. Your fears might be unfounded, unnecessary, or even irrational. Muster up the courage to follow God's call. It might not turn out as badly as you had feared! Many are those who finished leading their first Bible study, or who just handled a controversy, or changed jobs, and who said, "That wasn't as bad as I was afraid it would be!" When you courageously pursue your call, even when it strikes terror in your heart, you might be pleasantly surprised at how well it goes.

That courage I'm talking about is not merely something you find inside yourself, however. Maybe we'd better talk about that.

COURAGE, NOT SELF-RELIANCE

Moses had died and Joshua had inherited a difficult job. Following Moses and leading the Israelites would be a tough combination. But God said to him, "Be strong and courageous, for you are a super guy with a winning smile. And besides, this leadership thing is easy; it's a piece of cake."

No, of course that's not what God said. Rather, God said, *"Do not be terrified; do not be discouraged, for the LORD your God will be with you wherever you go"* (Joshua 1:9). God commissioned Joshua: "Be strong and courageous, for in every decision you make and every change you initiate and every conflict that erupts, I will be before you, behind you, and beside you."

I love what Calvin Miller wrote in *An Owner's Manual for the Unfinished Soul:* "The people of God do not always win, but they never lose alone."

On September 11, 2001, Todd Beamer and others on United Flight 93 so disrupted the hijackers' plans that the hijackers crashed the plane. And the everyday courage of those everyday heroes is matched by that of Beamer's young widow, Lisa Beamer. She has spoken often of the fact that we all have the potential to do courageous things, but she goes farther to say that human courage is sufficient only to a certain point. "If I were trying to hold my life together based on my human strength," she said, "I wouldn't get out of bed. I am so thankful to have my God-given strength and courage."

Please understand—Lisa Beamer is no superwoman. For a long time after Todd's death, she would find herself in the bedroom closet where his clothes still hung on the hangers and his softball cleats still sat on the floor. There she would weep and sometimes cry out to Todd, "I can't believe you did this to me!" She had her doubts and her fears and a hole in her heart. But she would wipe her face with one of Todd's T-shirts and she'd go on. Because of courage. Not mere human courage; rather, what she calls her *"God-given strength and courage."*

Truth is, there are hundreds of thousands of Lisa Beamers—people who aren't asked for interviews, and who get no publicity, yet who are heroes in God's eyes. People who know that the courage to follow a divine call is not about our own dogged determination. People who know that the courage of a Christ follower is the choice to believe that God is who He says He is, and that He is faithful to His promises.

The courage of the call is neither machismo, bravado, nor audacity. Real courage is a decision—a decision made sometimes by people who are shaking in their boots—that God who calls us won't fail us. The courage of the call is an outgrowth of faith. Brennan Manning wrote in *Ruthless Trust*:

> The reality of naked trust is the life of a pilgrim who leaves what is nailed down, obvious, and secure, and walks into the unknown without any rational explanation to justify the decision or guarantee the future. Why? Because God has signaled the movement and offered it his presences and his promise.

So be strong and courageous, for in every decision you make and every change you initiate and every conflict that erupts, the Creator of the Universe never will leave you and never will forsake you.

"ADAM" CONTINUED...

By the way, let me finish the story of Adam. Remember the boy Adam from the bungee jump at the beginning of this chapter?

When Adam came down from the platform, my daughter Brennan and I went over to ride the go-carts. While standing at the window to buy the tickets, I looked back and saw Adam standing with his family near the bungee tower. It looked like Adam was thinking again about jumping.

Brennan and I walked over and got in a long line. But I couldn't get my mind off Adam. Our line wound around until several minutes later I looked over and saw Adam sitting with his family. It looked like they were celebrating. I wondered if, maybe, he had jumped, so I told Brennan I'd be right back. I hurried over to see for myself. I didn't know him from Adam (of course he *was* Adam)—but I asked him, "Hey, man, did you jump?" And Adam answered with a broad smile, "Yes. Yes, I did!"

He'd been there before, and walked away. But on his second time out he mustered the courage to do that which, deep down in his heart, he wanted to do.

The man who advised Wanda Lee and prayed for her is right: **All the wisdom in the world is of little use unless we**

have the courage to act on it. My hunch is someone reading this has had the wisdom to discern God's call. If so, it's time to jump.

FAITH-ENOUGH-TO-
STICK-TO-IT-IVENESS

Resting is essential. Quitting,
however, is not an option.

Daniel Goleman suggests in his book of the same name that what he calls *Emotional Intelligence* is far more accurate in determining one's potential for success than is IQ (intelligence quotient). Goleman draws from extensive research and says that, among other things, that which sets apart the top performers in all fields is a dogged determination.

Scripture takes it a step farther, and says that a key to being an effective follower of Jesus is one's FQ— (faithfulness quotient). Not just grit and determination. But faithfulness.

The Greek word *pistis* may be translated "faith" or "faithfulness." A broader translation of *pistis* is "making faith a living reality in one's life." Faithfulness, therefore, means perseverance, but not *blind* perseverance, not mere stubborn determination. It is a perseverance based on confidence, certainty, and trust.

So faithfulness is stick-to-it-iveness based on faith. *Pistis* is faith-enough-to-stick-to-it-iveness. Faith enough to stick to our call when we're discouraged. Faith enough to stick to it when others are falling away. Faith enough to stick to it when there are questions for which there are no answers. Faith-enough-to-stick-to-it-iveness!

If I had one wish for call followers, it would be perseverance. There are so many issues that tempt us to throw in the towel. Countless are those who began in vocational ministry but are now doing something else. Many of them have left the church altogether. I realize God's call can change. As I said before, when our passions change and we develop different gifts, God might decide to use us in a different capacity. But it's hard for me to imagine that God has changed the assignments of so many.

The same is true of volunteers. A multitude of folks have fallen by the wayside. They have not merely moved to another ministry; they are not serving at all. Their gifts lie wasted, and needs go unmet. Spiritual warfare is raging and legions of Christian troops are AWOL.

Sometimes people don't stick with their spiritual commitment. Yet a recurring mandate in Scripture is for true believers to persevere to the end. The call to persevere probably will mean different things to different readers. Let's look at three thieves known to rob the Christian faith of good workers: burnout, doubt, and discouragement.

BURNOUT

You've heard people say they would rather burn out than rust out. Someone offered a great response to that: Who said those are the only choices? Call following does require a good work ethic. Running with our engines wide open, however, is not part of the deal.

Marshall Nelson, Ethyl Corporation's vice-president for

research and development and a member of Bon Air Baptist Church, took me on a tour of their facilities one day. In one wing of the building there are several automobile engines running. And running. And running. In fact, they never stop. These are experiments; the engines are automotive guinea pigs. The engineers run them, observe the effect that various fuel additives have on them, and keep them running until they just wear out.

Churches and other Christian organizations are a lot like Ethyl's research and development department. **We find a good engine—someone who serves faithfully and effectively—and we run them until they wear out.** I hope we who lead churches will wise up and treat people more humanely. We have got to do a better job at giving people permission to live balanced lives. Until we leaders improve at that, however, you are probably going to have to look out for yourself. The following are some ways to do that.

Find your place in the body. Scripture paints a picture of the church as Christ's body (see Romans 12). That beautiful image has varied applications. I believe it is helpful as we consider how to avoid burnout.

If you are a follower of Jesus, then you are a member of the body of Christ. You were created to function and thrive and to fulfill a role within that body. It's not only important to find a role, it must be the *right* role.

Do you remember Mr. Potato Head? He was a popular toy in my younger days and I think he made a comeback a few years ago. Mr. Potato Head was a potato-shaped little guy with holes where various body parts were to be placed, and the body parts were interchangeable. He was made for entertainment, and it was amusing to put the nose over on the side of his head and his eyes where his nose should be and his mouth where his eyes should be, and so on.

Hanging body parts in the wrong place was funny on Mr. Potato Head. Such mismatching, however, wouldn't be funny on a real, live body. And it's dysfunctional in the body of Christ. When we are in the wrong place, it is awkward and frustrating, and ministry doesn't get done well. Besides that, the body part burns out!

Have you ever tried to walk on your hands? Even if someone were to help you balance up there, you couldn't walk on your hands for long, for your hands weren't made for walking. That principle holds true in the body of Christ. We serve best when we serve in the place for which we were created.

Furthermore, you don't have to remain in a ministry that doesn't fit. Sure, all of us have to do things that are not fun for us. From time to time we pitch in to help our churches, for example, in projects that do not appeal to us but that simply need to be done. The bulk of our ministry, however, ought to be carried out in areas of our gifts and passions.

If in your quest to find your place you end up in the *wrong* place, or if you are in a ministry now that isn't right for you, then don't feel stuck. Feel free to speak to the leader of that ministry and be honest. Graciously tell him or her that you want to try another role. Don't languish and burn out in a role that doesn't fit.

Just admit it's not right. You won't be shipped to the Island of Misfit Toys. A good church family, or any Christian organization worth its salt, will help you find a ministry that *does* fit your callings, gifts, and passions. We would rather have you serving in your sweet spot than to have you burn out merely because we need a warm body in some position.

Take care of yourself. Finding your place in the body of Christ is one way to avoid burnout. Another important way to avoid being used up is simple self-care. Of course a critical component of self-care is *rest*. For highly motivated call followers, that is a tough one.

In his book titled *The Overload Syndrome*, Richard Swenson made a great point about how busy we are: "We send packages by Federal Express, use a long distance company called Sprint, manage our personal finances on Quicken, schedule our appointments on a DayRunner, diet with Slim Fast, and swim in trunks made by Speedo." In a fast-paced world like ours, we have to *choose* to rest!

Bruce Bass runs a crane company. In 2003 Hurricane Isabel blew through Richmond and, because the hurricane toppled thousands of trees, there was a heavy demand for cranes afterwards. A few months after the hurricane I asked Bruce if he'd gotten caught up. "Yes," he said, "but now we are concentrating on maintenance." They had been working almost around the clock to clean up the massive damage after the hurricane. After all that, their cranes needed some downtime to be cared for. Nonstop work is too much of a drain and strain on a crane.

The same is true for you. Many of us go and go until we either crack up, break down, cave in, or burn out. Like those cranes, sometimes responsibilities demand that we work a hectic schedule for a while, and even days off are a luxury we cannot afford during those rare crunch times. But we must build in time for breaks.

Learn to say no. Jesus knew how to say no. There is a fascinating story in Mark, chapter 1, about His willingness to decline invitations. In the city of Capernaum people lined up to see Jesus. Verse 33 says, "The whole town gathered at the door." Jesus healed many people and exorcised their demons. Because many had not yet been seen by Jesus, the next day promised another long line of needs. Early the next morning Jesus went off to be alone where He prayed. His disciples found him and reported, "Everyone is looking for you."

They expected him to jump up and get to work. But He told His disciples it was time to go to the next village. "I can preach there also," Jesus said. "That is why I have come." Our Lord turned down a good opportunity for ministry so that He could fully invest Himself in that to which He was called.

Jesus understood His mission, He set priorities, and He said no to His disciples' petition with the same confidence with which He often said yes. Some of us also need to understand our mission, set priorities, and learn to confidently say no to some of the requests for our services.

Confess the pridefulness of our busyness. Let's be candid; some of us are proud of our busyness. One of our favorite topics of conversation is how busy we are. We brag about our overloaded schedules, for being busy makes us feel needed and important.

The truth, however, is that when I think I'm too busy to rest, I'm actually being self-centered. I'm assuming that more depends on me than actually does. The kingdom of God would not collapse if you and I were to work a little less. Faith says, "I will obey the laws that God set forth and get the rest I need. I will trust Him for what does not get done."

Watch your Plimsoll line. I have learned that ships have a Plimsoll line—a marking on the cargo hull that designates how full the cargo hull can get before it endangers the ship. They can load and load and load cargo in the hull, but when the weight gets such that the Plimsoll line is below the water, the ship is in danger and some of the load must be removed. If not, the ship eventually will sink.

We all have our Plimsoll lines. And those who haven't learned to say no, or who feel obligated to do everything, or who somehow gain a feeling of importance by being involved in too many things, often load their hulls beyond the Plimsoll lines.

Don't overload; you'll sink. Different ships have different capacities, and they should carry only the load for which they were designed. The same is true of people, and you must be self-aware enough to know when you are near your limit.

That's why I have my "lop off" talk with the church staff from time to time. I encourage them to "lop off" something, so that they might concentrate more on that which (1) is in their area of giftedness, and (2) contributes the most to God's kingdom. We tend to accumulate more and more things to do. If we don't intentionally eliminate some of the responsibilities we tend to pick up along the way, soon we will be overloaded.

You have high and godly ambitions, but sunken ships carry little cargo. So watch your Plimsoll line.

Know that self-care is kingdom business too. Once I was invited to an important occasion—a Christian function. I supported the event and would have planned on being there, except for the fact that I was scheduled to officiate a ball game. I said to my friend who had invited me that I would not be able to attend because I was doing a football game. Believe it or not, those ball games are important to my self-care. It's good for me physically. It's good for me emotionally. It's recreation—re-creation—for me. (There's nothing like standing out in the cold letting people yell at me to recharge my batteries!)

This friend responded that he wished I'd request to be released from that game assignment so that I could come to this event. "This is kingdom business," he said. He wasn't being mean; he simply knew how important this event was and felt it crucial that I be there. I answered, "It is also kingdom business for me to take care of my mind and body." (The game got rained out, by the way, and I was able to attend the event. My friend jovially interpreted that as a sign from God as to where I was supposed to be that night.)

It *is* kingdom business to take care of yourself. That means finding a balance in your life, taking time to re-create, and making sure you have found *your* place in the body of Christ. Those are not superfluous issues; those are spiritual issues—kingdom business.

Those burned-out engines at Ethyl Corporation aren't getting anybody anywhere now. They lie in some scrap heap somewhere. Take care of yourself.

DOUBT

Not all perhaps, but most of us, have doubts from time to time.

- Doubts arise when we see Christians not acting very Christian.
- Doubts arise when bad things happen to good people.
- Doubts arise when we watch personal agendas supplant vision and mission.
- Doubts arise when people offer clichés and pat answers to our tough questions.
- Doubts sometimes arise for no identifiable reason.

And there are a couple of things we need to understand about doubt. First, doubts are not the same as unbelief. Doubts are usually the result of being troubled about something, perhaps the result of a traumatic experience or even of honest intellectual struggles. Unbelief, on the other hand is a willful decision—a choice not to believe. Second, doubts aren't necessarily a bad thing. Frederick Buechner called doubts "ants in the pants of faith"; and said of doubts, "They keep it awake and moving." Doubts can make us wrestle with our beliefs, to dig and investigate and ask, "Is mine a living faith?"

However, doubts can be debilitating. Doubts can overpower faith. Doubts can turn someone with honest questions into a skeptic, a cynic, or an agnostic. Faith-enough-to-stick-to-it-iveness requires the choice not to let that happen.

I'm not advocating a kind of blind faith that refuses to struggle with life's tough questions. However, faith is largely a matter of holding on. Holding on to faith means accepting that only God knows everything, and choosing to live with unanswerable questions.

Holding on to faith also means being obedient to what we believe is God's call for us, in spite of our doubts. In

C. S. Lewis's book, *The Screwtape Letters*, we find a collection of letters from an imaginary demon in hell (Screwtape) to an imaginary demon on earth (Wormwood). In one of the letters Screwtape writes, "Our cause is never more in danger than when a human...looks round upon a universe from which every trace of [God] seems to have vanished, asks why he has been forsaken, and still obeys."

Some of you are perhaps in the middle of a battle for your faith. I encourage you to hold on. You are not alone in your doubt. Jesus's 12 original call followers had their doubts too.

Matthew 28:16–17 says, *"Then the eleven disciples went to Galilee, to the mountain where Jesus had told them to go. When they saw him, they worshiped him; but some doubted."* I'd heard that wasn't the literal interpretation of that verse, so I got down the original Greek. (Actually, I got down my Greek New Testament that has the literal English translation right above it.) And what I'd heard was right. According to what I found, the verse literally reads, "And seeing him they worshipped him; they but doubted." (I know it reads oddly, but that is the literal translation.)

It doesn't say, "Most worshipped, but a couple, probably including Thomas, had their doubts." It says the worship offered by each of them was mixed with an element of doubt.

And these were the guys who'd seen Him appear through a locked door! These were the guys who'd seen the wounds in His hands and side. These were the guys who had shouted to the small band of Jesus followers: "He's alive! We've seen Him!" Yet they had their doubts. Everything was happening so fast.

That wasn't the last time people worshipped and doubted all at once. Every weekend in churches around the world people worship…and doubt. We sing songs of God's wonder-working power and wonder if He really does work wonders.

They worshipped; they but doubted.

My favorite prayer in the Bible is that of the father pleading with Jesus to heal his son. "Everything is possible for him who believes," Jesus told him. "I do believe," said the father, "help me overcome my unbelief." Jesus then healed his son.

That man was not the last one to pray with a shaky faith. Don't we pray sometimes and wonder, at least a little bit, if it's doing any good? Lord, we believe, but help our unbelief.

A few years ago, there was a popular movie, starring Denzel Washington and Whitney Houston, *The Preacher's Wife*. In the movie, God sent an angel (played by Washington) to help out a preacher and his wife.

A little boy was living with his grandmother just down the street from the preacher and his family. The youngster's best friend was the pastor's son. In a moving scene the little boy was being taken from his grandmother to live with someone else. His grandmother loved him, and provided a good home for him, and the little boy was happy. But someone had inaccurately judged her unfit to care for the little boy, and so he was being taken somewhere else.

The little fellow was brokenhearted. As the car carrying him drove away, his dejected face appeared in the rear window of the car, and he waved sadly good-bye to his best friend, the pastor's son.

The angel looked up toward heaven and confessed, "I know You have a master plan, but sometimes You're hard to figure."

The angel's candid words to God express the confusion that most of us have experienced. How many times has one of us said, or at least thought, that very same thing: "God, I know You have a master plan, but sometimes You're hard to figure"?

There are basically two kinds of faith: the kind of faith that says, "When all is going well I trust God"; and the kind that says, "Even though God sometimes is hard to figure, I believe He can be trusted, and I will obey His call."

DISCOURAGEMENT

One of the most difficult things about call following can be dispiriting input from those around us. From Laurie Beth Jones I learned the WOWSE concept. WOWSE—With or Without Someone Else. Jones wrote in *Jesus CEO*,

> WOWSE became a vital affirmation for me when I was starting my own company. Like too many others, I had tried to get assistance from banks and was continually turned down. Every time I was rejected, I would say to myself, "WOWSE," which means, "With Or Without Someone Else." "I will build this company with or without someone else," I would repeat to myself as I licked my wounds.

Some of you know what it is like to ache for, but not receive, the approval and confidence of your peers. Some of you might be starving for a word of encouragement from someone whose opinion you value. For some of you, perhaps, it has been even worse. Some of you have been shot down, dragged down, put down, cut down, worn down, and beaten down.

Some of you, perhaps, have expressed a sense of call, but

you are being discouraged from the pursuit of that call. You might have to do what is right and follow your God-given call with or without someone else.

King David practiced WOWSE. A recurring story within the story during David's life was his willingness to fulfill his calling despite the naysayers, detractors, critics, hecklers, and disbelievers.

David's big brother distrusted him. *"I know how conceited you are and how wicked your heart is; you came down only to watch the battle"* (1 Samuel 17:28.)

David's king disparaged him. *"You are not able to go out against this Philistine and fight him; you are only a boy"* (1 Samuel 17:33).

David's enemy despised him. *"He [Goliath] looked David over and saw that he was only a boy, ruddy and handsome, and he despised him"* (1 Samuel 17:42).

David's wife (one of them) deserted him. Michal assisted David in escaping when Saul turned on David and wanted to kill him. When confronted, however, she lied: *"He threatened me. He said, 'Help me out of here or I'll kill you'"* (1 Samuel 19:18 *The Message*).

David's army detested him. *"David was greatly distressed because the men were talking of stoning him; each was bitter in his spirit because of his sons and daughters"* (1 Samuel 30:6).

David's son defied him. *"Absalom sent secret messengers throughout the tribes of Israel to say, 'As soon as you hear the sound of the trumpets, then say, "Absalom is king in Hebron"'"* (2 Samuel 15:10).

David's heckler denounced him. *"As he cursed, Shimei said, 'Get out, get out, you man of blood, you scoundrel!*

The LORD has repaid you for all the blood you shed in the household of Saul, in whose place you have reigned. The LORD has handed the kingdom over to your son Absalom. You have come to ruin because you are a man of blood!'" (2 Samuel 16:7–8).

David's big brother distrusted him. David's king disparaged him. David's enemy despised him. His wife deserted him and his army detested him. His son defied him and his heckler denounced him. But they could not derail him.

David knew he was called by God. He had an unshakable sense of call, of direction. He had a "purpose-driven life." Acts 13:36 tells us, *"When David had served God's purpose in his own generation, he fell asleep."* He fulfilled God's purposes for him in spite of all those who didn't believe in him—and in spite of those who downright opposed him.

Some of you are going to have to move on too. Even if people distrust you, disparage you, despise you, desert you, detest you, defy you, or denounce you, don't let them derail you. Some of you are going to have to move on with or without someone else. It's time for you to talk to God and say, "Now, God, I'm Your child, and nothing less. So I'm going to accomplish Your purposes for me. I'm going to be who You called me to be. I'm going to take my place in Your family and fulfill my role in Your mission."

Psalm 139:14 says, *"You knit me together in my mother's womb."* When God strung your DNA, like a master jeweler strings pearls for an exquisite necklace, He had *you* in mind. So be who God created you to be, and do what God created you to do, with or without someone else.

By the way, do you know where Laurie Beth Jones got her WOWSE idea? From Jesus. It's in her book, *Jesus CEO.*

It's not a Christian book per se; it's a book for business leaders that uses Jesus as a model for leadership.

She noted that Jesus was faithful to His mission whether or not he had the approval and confidence of others. Even Jesus had to overcome the voices of dissent and discouragement. Mark 3:21 says, *"When his family heard about this [Jesus's teaching and the response of the crowd], they went to take charge of him, for they said, 'He is out of his mind.'"* But Jesus kept marching to the Cross.

John 7:5 says, *"Even his own brothers did not believe in him."* But Jesus kept marching to the Cross.

Peter reprimanded Jesus for talking of dying. And he kept on marching to the Cross.

Religious leaders demonized Jesus for talking about being the Messiah. And yet Jesus kept on marching to the Cross.

Many of His followers deserted Him when the demands got tough. And Jesus kept on marching to the Cross.

The Roman soldiers mocked Jesus. And He kept on marching to the Cross.

You are going to have to courageously follow what you believe in your heart to be the leadership of God's Spirit... with or without someone else.

Don't let anyone talk you out of your sweater. I am a fan of the University of Alabama Crimson Tide. Do you know why I'm an Alabama fan? Because of Dewayne and a sweater.

When I was a little boy—probably seven or eight—I had a sweater. I wore it to church only once, and refused to wear it again. My mother bought that sweater for me. It was orange and blue and had the letters *AU,* for Auburn University, written on it.

Dewayne, who went to our church, was an avid University of Alabama fan. When he saw my Auburn sweater he nearly had a stroke. Dewayne (two years older than I) absolutely hated Auburn, and he made me feel awful for wearing that sweater.

I was too little to know or care about Alabama or Auburn. But I did know this: I wanted Dewayne, and the other kids, to like me. I knew how much it mattered to me that Dewayne, and the other kids, approved of me. So I became an Alabama Crimson Tide fan and ditched the Auburn sweater. (I sometimes wear an Auburn cap that an Auburn alum gave me, but only when I'm working in the yard. And I'd probably yank it off if I saw Dewayne turn in my driveway.)

We are born with a feeling that what others think is somehow awfully important. We have that innate desire to please other people, to make people like us. Of course sometimes that gets us into trouble, for we do things that violate our values and God's standards in order to get the approval of other people. I dare say that more people (of all ages) have been led astray by peer pressure than anything else. The desire to please other people, when unchecked, can be destructive. In fact, if you and I try to adjust our lives according to the expectations of others we will go nuts. And we will forget who we really are. Follow the call, not the crowd.

Paul asked, "*You were running a good race. Who cut in on you and kept you from obeying the truth?*" (Galatians 5:7). What a poignant image that is: A runner is running along in the long-distance race, being careful to stay in her lane, when out of nowhere someone cuts in on her. The runner is bumped and sidetracked. Her attention is diverted from the race to the distraction of this strange woman who has wandered into her lane.

For the call follower, often it is burnout, doubt, or discouragement that has cut in and knocked him or her out of the race. Don't let that happen to you. Live so that you may declare at the finish line, *"I have fought the good fight. I have finished the race. I have kept the faith"* (2 Timothy 4:7).

When Keri and I were in the process of being appointed as missionaries, our evaluations included a session with a psychiatrist. I remember two things about that interview. First, he asked which of us is the most organized, then sat back and took notes as Keri and I, uh, discussed that question. Second, the psychiatrist said, "Tell me about your father."

I remember the words that jumped from my lips without my having to think about the question, **"My father is solid; he is consistent; he is the same man now as when I was a little fellow."**

My late father had a sixth-grade education. But he could have gotten a PhD in perseverance.

He was faithful to his marriage. His marriage to my mother was his second; but for 40-something years, until death parted them, he was a one-woman man.

He was faithful to the church, though the church sometimes disappointed him.

He was faithful to the careful and daily study of the Bible, though there were many things he didn't understand.

In his late 30s, after having lived a wayward life, he decided to follow Jesus. A part of that decision was not to turn back.

He was a call follower with faith-enough-to-stick-to-it-iveness. One day, when someone asks my kids to describe their father, I want them to be able to say the same about me.

It's one thing to look at the COMPASS through ambitious eyes. It's quite another to persevere come what may. Let's stick to it.

Within most of us lives the tension between a selfish desire for recognition and a selfless commitment to God's mission in the world. I love the way Robert Schnase describes it: "Football players cheer for the other players on their team and want to win the championship. On the other hand, every football player dreams of scoring the game-winning touchdown."

Ministry is not about self-promotion. Jeremiah challenged us: *"Should you then seek great things for yourself? Seek them not"* (Jeremiah 45:5). About that verse J. Oswald Sanders wrote, "The prophet was not condemning all ambition as sinful, but he was pointing to selfish motivation that makes ambition wrong—'great things *for yourself.*'"

Pride is a sin against which the call follower must always be on guard. J. Oswald Sanders said in *Spiritual Leadership,*

When a person rises in position, as happens to leaders in the church, the tendency to pride also increases. If not checked, the attitude will disqualify the person from further advancement in the kingdom of God, for "the Lord detests the proud of heart" (Proverbs 16:5).

ASSIGNED TO THE VALLEY

Aspirations are not intrinsically evil. They do, however, come with inherent dangers. Those of us who are "driven" and intent on doing significant things with our lives have a tendency to like the spotlight. If we aren't careful, we will forget that it's not all about us. **The line between God's glory and our egotism sometimes gets blurred, and it's easy to forget whose kingdom we are building.**

I sometimes forget that it's not about me. I have to be alert to my tendency toward selfish motives in service. But from those times when I have chosen not to seek the spotlight I have learned that there is a real peace, a deep satisfaction, a sense of well-being, that comes from letting someone else get the credit for something. Besides that, as someone said, "It's amazing what can happen when no one cares who gets the credit."

How many of you know the name John Leland? Probably not many.

But John Leland is an important American, and of particular significance to those who value religious liberty. Leland was largely responsible for the First Amendment to our Constitution, the guarantee of religious liberty in what we call the Bill of Rights. But James Madison gets the credit for that, and here's why.

John Leland and James Madison were running for election to the Virginia Constitutional Convention—the gathering of elected Virginians to consider ratifying the new Constitution of the United States. In Orange County, Virginia, the two men met. Leland shared with James Madison his deep conviction that the guarantee of religious liberty should be a part of the US Constitution. Madison was so convinced by Leland's argument that Madison pledged to fight for freedom of religion should he be elected. At that point, Leland withdrew from the race and threw all his votes to Madison. Madison was elected and, because of Madison, the guarantee of religious liberty is the First Amendment to our Constitution.

Leland was willing to become a footnote in American history for the sake of the cause. His personal convictions were more important than his political ambitions. The country's future was more important than his stature. Leland was content to let Madison get the credit for the sake of our nation.

Indeed, it's amazing what can happen when no one cares who gets the credit.

I want to become more like John Leland. That also means I'd like to be more like Joshua. Joshua was content to take his place in the shadows—when the spotlight was on Joshua's boss.

We are acquainted with Joshua's spectacular, and very public, acts of courage. First there was the felling of the wall of Jericho. Then there was the crossing of the Jordan on dry ground. Then there was the time Joshua prayed and the sun stood still. **Why was Joshua able to do the right thing when the world was looking? Because he was accustomed to doing the right thing when *no one* was looking.**

Exodus 17:9 reads, *"Moses said to Joshua, 'Choose some of our men and go out to fight the Amalekites. Tomorrow I will stand on top of the hill with the staff of God in my hands.'"* I can just imagine Joshua asking Moses to repeat that. Maybe Joshua said, "Mr. Moses, are you telling me I'm assigned to the valley? It sure sounded to me like you said I was to go down in the valley and fight the Amalekites and you were going to stand on the mountain holding the rod." That is exactly what Moses had said.

So the next day found Joshua down in the valley risking his neck, leading charges and dodging spears, while Moses was standing up there with his hands in the air. Which picture do you think made the morning paper the next day? Joshua in the trenches, or Moses in that Charlton Heston-esque stance on the mountaintop?

When Moses was up on the hill striking that memorable pose, Joshua was confident and humble enough to fight down in the trenches, out of the spotlight. That makes Joshua one of Scripture's most important role models for call followers. **Great call followers are willing to serve in the valley.**

STEPPING-STONES ARE
FOR CROSSING STREAMS

The "stepping-stone" mentality has no place among call followers. If we truly believe that we are where we are by divine mandate, then who are we to actively seek another position— a position that carries, in our opinion, higher status? Scripture says that it is God who determines our upward or downward move on our culture's status ladder (Psalm 75:6–7). Call following implies just what it says—*following a call*—not pursuing our personal (and perhaps self-seeking) goals.

Does that mean you should never accept an invitation to a project or organization that requires greater responsibility or involves more people than where you presently serve? Of course not. As some have said, our abilities are like Japanese carp; they grow in proportion to the size of their environment.

Does call following mean you should never submit your résumé for a position that fits your expanding interests and growing skills? I don't think so. Often experience in one role does prepare us for a role that is more complex.

However, calculated moves and self-centered decisions are never appropriate, whether we are talking about a volunteer role in the congregation, a paid position with a church, a parachurch organization, a missions agency, or a new job opening at the office. As with most decisions, when it comes to the consideration of opportunities before us, right and wrong boils down to motive.

Ladder climbing and stone-stepping seem to me particularly objectionable when it comes to ministry positions, be they volunteer or paid. I think all lay and vocational ministers ought to read Robert Schnase's book, *Ambition in Ministry: Our Struggle with Success, Achievement, and Competition.* Schnase does a great job of pointing out the positive aspect of ambition: "A fundamental need to make a positive difference, to expand into our environment, to engage others and take up new challenges—all this comes from the stirring of ambition in our souls." On the other hand, Schnase observes that ambition "also fosters fierce competition, unhappiness, disillusionment, and isolation."

Effective ministry happens, writes Schnase, when we recognize our potential for self-centeredness and, with the help of God's Spirit, ride herd on it. When we learn to live with the tension, never giving in to the temptation to make it all about us, we can serve with joy and make a great contribution to the world.

A key is realizing that our self-validation rests in our being valued by God, not in performance and accolades. Personal value is a gift from our Creator, not something we earn or even enhance by landing more impressive roles and titles. Recognition of that truth will allow us to view our present calling as a gift from God, not a stepping-stone to something else.

Hence ambition, striving for excellence, and the challenge of reaching our potential are not necessarily sinful. We simply must be constantly aware of our tendency to pursue self-promotion. It also is helpful to remember that our sinful minds will play tricks on us—clothing our selfish ambition in the garb of "a greater challenge."

Let's wrap this section up with observations by the eminent missions leader, J. Oswald Sanders, who weighed in on this matter of ambition in his classic book, *Spiritual Leadership*:

> No doubt, Christians must resist a certain kind of ambition and rid it from their lives. But we must also acknowledge other ambitions as noble, worthy, and honorable. It is motivation that determines ambition's character. Our Lord never taught against the urge to high achievement, but He did expose and condemn unworthy motivation....
>
> Jesus taught that ambition that centers on the self is wrong....The word *ambition* comes from a Latin word meaning "campaigning for promotion." The phrase suggests...social visibility and approval, popularity, peer recognition, the exercise of authority over others. Ambitious

people, in this sense, enjoy the power that comes with money and authority. Jesus had no time for such ego-driven ambitions.

PRIDE AND JEALOUSY

If there had been a "Who's Who" at Rehoboth High School around 1010 B.C., Saul would have been voted Most Likely to Succeed. He was tall, confident, and charismatic. A natural-born leader. Chosen by God Himself to be the king of Israel. Saul had it all.

But let's fast-forward to the end of his life. On the closing page of the Book of 1 Samuel, Saul lies in a pool of blood and self-pity. Just a moment earlier, in a last-ditch effort to save face, he fell on his sword and intentionally took his own life.

What went so terribly wrong? Well, as my dad would have said, "He got too big for his britches." Saul became guilty of pride, and was consumed by pride's first cousin, jealousy.

Pride is not the satisfaction you feel when your son or daughter walks across the graduation stage, or when a raise gives due recognition to your hard work and loyalty, or when you get an A on a paper that you worked hard on while others were playing.

Pride is obsession with one's self. Pride is the distorted opinion that history is a movie with me as the star, and everyone else as supporting characters. The fancy word for that is *megalomania*! Megalomania is an overexaggerated sense of one's importance. Saul was megalomaniacal. **Saul was a megalomaniac!**

That kind of pride inevitably results in jealousy. The proud person is threatened, and becomes jealous, when someone else gets ahead, or receives applause. A proud person cannot stand to share the spotlight.

This became Saul's downfall. Saul was basking in the spotlight when the youthful hero named David burst onto the scene. The adoration of Saul's subjects began to shift from Saul to the brave, young champion. After David killed Goliath, word of David's daring deed spread. There was a big parade and Saul, from the reviewing stand, heard the women sing a song they'd made up: "Saul has slain thousands." And Saul said, "They like me! They really like me!" But then they sang the next stanza: "And David has slain *tens* of thousands." Saul's royal bubble burst.

From that song on, Saul was consumed with his resentment of David. Saul was so full of himself that he could not stand to hear David's name cheered. The envious monarch turned on David and wasted the rest of what could have been a wonderful life chasing David around trying to kill the young shepherd-turned-giant-killer. Saul spent his last, tormented years consumed by a neurotic obsession. He eventually fell on his sword and died.

Pride was Saul's ruin. And if we aren't careful, we will allow pride to be *our* ruin. We might not end up falling on our swords, but pride has destroyed many a good life. And there are probably those of us who have our Davids—those we consider our rivals—those of whom we are jealous.

So how do we defeat pride in our own lives? It won't be easy. Someone suggested that our pride won't die until 15 minutes after our hearts stop beating. But here are some practical and biblical steps to minimizing pride and its second cousin, jealousy.

Toot not thine own horn. Proverbs 27:2 tells us to *"let another praise you, and not your own mouth; someone else, and not your own lips."* It's a funny thing. The harder we try to impress people, the less impressed they usually are. Most of us are drawn to people with a quiet confidence—those who don't have the need to parade their pedigrees or revel in their résumés.

Maybe you've heard the saying, "He that tooteth not his own horn, the same shall not be tooted." Then let it not be tooted. Not having it tooted at all is better than pridefully tooting it ourselves.

Content yourself with the shadows. Philippians 2:3–4 teaches us to *"do nothing out of selfish ambition or vain conceit, but in humility consider others better than yourself. Each of you should look not only to your own interests, but also to the interests of others."* A conscious decision to let others receive the attention is tough for most of us. Someone asked the famous conductor Leonard Bernstein what was the most difficult instrument to play. He answered, "Second fiddle. I can get plenty of folks who want to play *first* violin, but to find someone who will play *second* violin with enthusiasm is a real problem!" Likewise, the Oak Ridge Boys sang, "Everybody wants to be the lead singer in the band."

But let's choose to let others be the lead singers and get the credit. Let's develop the habit of pointing to the accomplishments of other people, especially those we are tempted to envy. It won't be easy, but when the second violinist can praise the first violinist, when the backup shortstop can praise the starting shortstop, and when the one who didn't get the job can praise the one who did—when the Sauls can praise the Davids—then we have gone a long way toward slaying the dragon of pride.

Let God "use" your pride. In the hymn "God of Grace and God of Glory" appears this wonderful line: "Bend our pride to Thy control." When I heard those lines I almost immediately remembered a conversation that I had back in college.

Cindy Walker was a friend of Keri's and mine at Samford University. She was a missionary kid, having grown up in Africa, and a very wise young woman. One day I confessed to Cindy that I felt like I was the wrong one to be a minister. "I struggle with the wrong motives," I told her. "Being the leader feels good to me, sometimes for the wrong reasons. And when I'm in front of people I tend to focus on what they think of *me.*" Cindy answered, "The desire to lead can be a useful means of serving God. It just has to be channeled in the right direction."

I still struggle with the sin I confessed to Cindy. I wish I were over it, but I'm not. All the while I'm writing about the dangers of pride there is part of me that sure hopes you think I'm a good writer! Yet I continually pray that God will "bend my pride to His control," and turn my potential weakness into a strength. Maybe you will join me in that struggle. For example, maybe you will pray, "God, I like for people to like me, so bend my pride to Your control; help me to be friendly to people who need a friend."

"God, I like to feel smart, so bend my pride to Your control; provide for me opportunities, perhaps to teach a Bible study class, in which my intellectual abilities can be used for Your purposes."

"God, I like to feel needed, so bend my pride to Your control; use that part of me that can be selfish in order to truly meet people's needs."

The desire to excel is not necessarily a curse, as long as it is directed appropriately. I think that is what Jesus was implying when He said, "If anyone wants to be first, he must be the very last, and the servant of all" (Mark 9:35).

Think neither too highly, nor too lowly, of yourself. Romans 12:3 teaches us how to do this rightly: *"For by the grace given me I say to every one of you: Do not think of yourself more highly than you ought, but rather think of yourself with sober judgment, in accordance with the measure of faith God has given you."* The opposite of pride is not self-deprecation or self-hatred. It is a realistic acknowledgment of our weaknesses and strengths, and our relationship with our Creator.

John Ortberg says, in *If You Want to Walk on Water*, there is an old story among the Hasidic Jews in which everybody has to wear a coat with two pockets. In one pocket is a note from God that reads: "You are nothing but one of millions upon millions of grains of sand in the universe." In the other pocket God's note reads, "I made the universe just for you." These two notes would encourage sober judgment of ourselves.

Look for buckets to empty. One of the most personally moving stories I've heard was told to me by a stately Nigerian man, a retired school principal, Mr. Ben Oke. Mr. Oke was our friend and language teacher when we lived in Nigeria.

This incident took place back around 1950, when Nigeria was still a colony of England—when white people were treated like VIPs, when missionaries were treated like princes, and when educators were treated like kings. Raymond Brothers was all three—a white missionary who was the principal of the Baptist boarding school for boys that Mr. Oke attended as a young man—so the pedestal on which Brothers was placed was high above the common person. Furthermore, from all I've heard about Raymond Brothers, he was a very gifted man.

My retired Nigerian friend, Mr. Oke, explained that at this boarding school they did not yet have toilets. Rather, every student had a bucket. (Forgive me for what might appear uncouth or crude. I am not trying to be sensational, only to illustrate an important point.) Each student used his own bucket and placed the bucket with the others in a particular location on campus.

One man from the town had the job of cleaning those buckets. It's obvious what a demeaning, dehumanizing job that was, and where, on the social ladder, people must have perceived him to be.

But one Monday the man who cleaned the buckets did not show up for work. A very distasteful situation developed. On Tuesday he didn't come, nor did he come on Wednesday or Thursday. Obviously, the state of affairs was growing more and more unsavory. Friday, then Saturday, rolled around and there was no one to clean up the buckets. We can only imagine how bad the conditions were by then.

Then, on Sunday night, the students scattered across the town and countryside to help in various church services as was required by the school. Mr. Oke, the one telling me the story, explained that he was one of the last ones to return that night. He said that when he entered the campus it was like walking into a funeral home; he thought someone had died. The mood was somber and all the students were very solemn.

Ben Oke asked what was wrong, and a fellow student

soberly reported, "While we were gone, Rev. Brothers cleaned our buckets."

What seems admirable to us was more than admirable there. It was unimaginable in that setting. Those students were taken aback, shocked, and humbled, that a person of such stature as Rev. Brothers cared about them so deeply that he was willing to lower himself and do the unthinkable. He loved them enough to condescend to clean their buckets.

That sounds a lot like Jesus, who *"being in the very nature God, did not consider equality with God something to be grasped, but made himself nothing, taking the very nature of a servant"* (Philippians 2:6–7).

Maybe there are some buckets around where you live your life. Tasks that don't gain you recognition. Interruptions that ruin your schedule. People who can't help you get ahead in your career, yet who could use a friend, and who are of great value to God.

If we would clean a few buckets, people might just see Jesus in us. **If we are not ready to do thankless, undignified work that is "beneath us," we are not quite ready to follow God's call.**

Sometimes our compasses point to the valley, where we fight alongside Joshua while others stand up with Moses on the mountain. But that shouldn't bother us; there is a lot to be said for valley ministry. A lot of battles are won there. A lot of characters are shaped there. A lot of calls are refined there. So don't demand a reassignment if you find yourself in the valley. And don't spend too much time staring enviously at the one up on the mountainside. Call out to him and tell him he's doing a good job. Then grab a sword; the Amalekites are coming.

HANDLING THE REALITIES

11

*Even strict attention to the compass
is no assurance of smooth sailing.*

Paul wrote to Timothy, a young, missional leader, and encouraged him to *"always be steady, endure suffering"* (2 Timothy 4:5 RSV). Reflecting on those words, John MacArthur wrote in *Ashamed of the Gospel,* "No ministry of any value comes without pain."

Most who read this will not undergo the serious persecution that our brothers and sisters in some parts of the world endure, yet we certainly will encounter irritations, aggravations, and complications along the way. Surprising to many is the fact that those frustrations come even if you are in the center of God's will. Don't confuse the center of God's will with the eye of the hurricane. In the eye of the hurricane everything is calm; **in the center of God's will the weather can get rough at times.**

The following are some of the disturbances you might have to endure.

You will work alongside people with whom you disagree.
When I was pastor in Upton, Kentucky, we celebrated the

90th anniversary of the church. In preparation for that, I waded through church minutes, looking for anecdotes. One of my favorite stories came from the days when the first church house was constructed, back in 1896. In that year, Jim Scaggs was a little boy going to school at the Lucas Grove School, which sat next to the land where the Lucas Grove Baptist Church was being built. Scaggs later wrote in church records that, during school, he would sit and look out the window, watching church members working on the building. I can just imagine the teacher now, "Jimmy, you quit looking out that window and pay attention to the multiplication tables!") When he wrote about watching them build the church, he made special note (with no explanation) of the fact that some of the workers had on silver hats and some had on gold hats.

Why, I thought, would it be such a big deal for people with silver hats and gold hats to be working together? I looked into our nation's history and found that, in 1896, when the church building was under construction, there was a presidential race between William McKinley (Republican) and William Jennings Bryan (Democrat). There was an acrimonious disagreement over whether US currency would be based on silver or gold. Democrats were fighting for silver; Republicans were fighting for gold. It was a bitter dispute which split friends and families, and people wore hats to display which side they were on. Yet there they were—people who felt so strongly about the issue that they came with their gold and silver hats on—sawing and hammering, handing each other tools and lumber, working side by side to build a church. They felt strongly about an issue that could have divided them, yet they felt *more* strongly about the mission that united them.

I can just about guarantee that if you get serious about joining God in what He is doing in the world, you will have to work alongside people with whom you disagree. Many denominations are in turmoil, so people who are in different camps are going to be thrown together from time to time. In those situations, missional Christ followers are willing to set aside their differences for the sake of God's work. **Missional people are people who feel strongly about some issues that could divide them, yet who feel more strongly about the mission that unites them.**

Not so long ago I attended a memorial service for a wonderful Christian gentleman whom everyone knew was opposed to the direction of his denomination. One of the four speakers at that service was a close friend and fellow church member of the deceased—a gentleman who openly *supports* the way his denomination has headed. The two men had strong and conflicting opinions about something important to them both. Yet each of them was *more* passionate about their church and its outreach ministries; their common zeal for missions superseded their differences over a denomination's leanings.

It's one thing to migrate toward people with whom we are most compatible. It's another thing to be closed-minded and hardheaded. I hope you will know the joy of working with people who wear different hats.

You will wonder if you're doing any good. Most of us wonder from time to time if we are making any difference in the world. A youth volunteer will hear shocking stories about the Saturday night behavior of kids who know all the answers in their Sunday morning Bible study class. A counselor will hear of the relapse of a client whom the counselor believed had made great strides. A schoolteacher will look into the eyes of kids who seem to be getting no support outside of the classroom and fear that these kids have little hope. A pastor will pray and work and see very little fruit from his labors. A missionary will mentor a new believer only to have that supposed convert return to his previous false gods. A physician will write one more prescription for an anti-depressant and fear that he is just putting bandages on people's broken lives.

You will question, "Is what I am doing making a difference at all?" Well, I want you to hear one of my favorite stories.

Fred Craddock came to speak in chapel when I was a seminary student. He told of his first pastorate—a little country church in which he wondered if he was making much of a difference. His sermons, he said, weren't much to listen to. And there was this one little girl who never paid attention. She was constantly fidgeting. Up in Mom's or Dad's lap, down in the floor, coloring or chatting or crying. And when he moved from that church, Craddock thought, "That little girl hasn't heard a word I've said."

Two decades passed, and he was called back to do the funeral of that same little girl's father. After the service he went to the family's home for a meal. The little girl, now a young woman, sat across the table from Fred Craddock. "Brother Fred," she said, "Do you know what got me through the grief of my daddy's death? It was the words you said in a sermon you preached on the Lord's Supper when you were the pastor here."

Craddock didn't remember that sermon, or what he'd said. And he thought the little girl hadn't heard anything he'd preached when he was pastor. Yet his words had been meaningful to her in a dark moment of her life.

Craddock was speaking to encourage us—the young ministers there—and throughout his story he repeated a three-word phrase that has come to mean a great deal to me. In his unique, high-pitched voice he'd say, "You never know! You never know!"

I hope you will file this away in your spirit somewhere, no matter what your ministry. When you wonder if any good is coming from your work for God, well, you never know!

You will get in over your head. Once two men were sitting on the front porch of the general store. One was a large, strapping, muscular fellow. The other was a thin little guy. They were talking about bear hunting. The little guy said to his big buddy, "If I were as big as you, I'd go out there and get me a big ole bear."

The big fellow paused thoughtfully and answered simply, "There's plenty o' little bears in the woods."

If you are a bit nervous about ministry, and worried that you will get in over your head, you might want to start with the little bears. There are bears that you can wrestle in these woods. You don't have to start with the grizzlies. You can take on a cub or two until you get the hang of it.

Yet there are, quite frankly, a lot of big bears that need wrestling. The bottom line is that eventually you will find yourself in a tussle with one of them. **It's not a matter of what if you get in over your head. You *will* get in over your head.** If you "attempt great things [for God], and expect great things [from God]," as William Carey, the father of modern missions, urged you to do, then you will find yourself in various situations for which you feel underqualified. That's not a bad thing, however. There is a lot to learn when we feel like we aren't up to the task to which we've been called.

Here's the big truth for folks who find themselves wrestling big bears: **Work out of God's strength, not your own.** (*"If anyone serves, he should do it with the strength God provides"* [1 Peter 4:11].)

"I can do all things," wrote the missionary Paul, *"through Christ who strengthens me"* (Philippians 4:13). You can too, for as soon as Christ commissioned us He promised he would be with us until the end of the age. His Spirit indwells and empowers you.

You will find that a church sometimes looks better from the pew than from the church office. Once a friend of our family's, a faithful member of her church, took a position as a church secretary. She was delighted to be on the "inside" at church. Shortly thereafter, however, I was comforting her, encouraging her, and reassuring her that everything was going to be all right. All she ever had seen was the church at worship; she'd never seen the church during the in-between times. What she saw behind the scenes was not always encouraging.

Earlier I mentioned that our church has invited some of our church members to take major roles on our paid staff. That seems to be a trend among larger churches, and there are a lot of advantages to that. One of the disadvantages to that practice is that **when one looks behind the civility of Sunday mornings, church people are, well, people, and that can be disappointing.**

At times there are undercurrents of conflict of which

the typical worshipper would not even be aware. The lay church leader knows it, though. At times families that appear perfect aren't. The people in the seats next to them on Sunday mornings don't know that. The staff member knows it, though. There are some church staffs that are plagued by interpersonal conflict. Most people who aren't privy to the behind-the-curtain world of the church aren't going to know that. But new staff members sometimes are disappointed by their colleagues' behavior.

Both salaried church staff members and volunteer leaders experience the occasionally unflattering side of things. Anyone who gets involved deeply in a church, or just about any Christian organization, is likely to experience some level of disappointment. Sometimes discussions over church finances, for instance, can get tense. Sometimes people get testy when their pet programs are challenged, or change is introduced. Some folks engage in what one song calls a "stained glass masquerade," and outside the sanctuary those folks can be challenging.

Don't get me wrong; I highly recommend the life of a church staff member, and finding your place of leadership in the body of Christ is one of the most fulfilling things you ever will do. Don't be surprised, however, if the church seems less idyllic from the inside. The church really is a wonderful place, and it is the body of Christ. The church is the primary channel through which God is unleashing His redeeming love to the world. The church, however, unlike its Lord, isn't perfect.

Don't take yourself too seriously. The Bible says that three of Job's friends heard about his tragedies and came to comfort him. When they first arrived, according to Job 2:12, they could hardly recognize him. Norman Patterson and I know how Job's friends felt. During my first pastorate Norman (a deacon) and I went to visit one of the church members, Maudie Vance, in the hospital.

Poor Maudie. We didn't even recognize her. She was much paler and much thinner than the last time we'd seen her. Why, except for the white hair, she did not look at all like the Maudie we knew. Norman and I gave each other a pitiful, knowing glance, as if to say without speaking a word, "Poor Maudie; she won't be with us much longer."

We tried to carry on a conversation with her, but she was so bad off she didn't even seem to know us. We mentioned names of her friends and family but she said over and over again, "I don't believe I know him or her." Bless her heart, Maudie didn't even recognize the names of those closest to her.

Then the woman who belonged in the other bed of that semiprivate room stepped out of the restroom...giggling. She apparently had been listening in on our conversation with this poor soul in the bed, and somehow found it funny.

The odd thing was that the woman coming out of the restroom laughing looked a lot like Maudie. She, well, she looked more like Maudie than the woman in the bed. In fact, the woman coming out of the restroom *was* Maudie! I still don't know who the poor woman was with whom Norman and I had carried on that long and awkward conversation.

Maudie thought that was the funniest thing she'd seen in a long time. She loved to repeat that story. Even Norman and I have gotten a lot of laughs out of that. I don't see Norman now more than once every few years, but it seems that every time we are together we tell that story and howl.

It is certainly appropriate to take your call seriously. But don't take *yourself* too seriously. **If you can't laugh at yourself, the call of God can become awfully burdensome.**

If you engage in God's mission, you will experience irritations, aggravations, and complications. You might as well accept, even embrace, that fact. Norman Vincent Peale once said, **"When you see a problem coming down the road, holler, 'Hello, Problem! Where have you been? I've been training for you all my life!'"**

PEACEMAKING AND "PEACEFAKING"

12

The family of God is a tight-knit family. Sometimes it might seem we are knit too tightly. Basil Pennington rightly observed: "We are like a bunch of porcupines trying to huddle together for warmth who are always driven apart out of fear of the wound we can inflict upon each other with our quills."

For those who follow God's call, the bumps in the road are not limited to irritations, aggravations, and complications. You might face fairly significant criticism and conflict. Some of you might be in the middle of it right now.

Anyone who holds a compass and declares, "This is the way I believe we should go," is going to be criticized. Robert E. Lee once declared, "We've made a terrible mistake! We've placed all our worst generals in the fields, and we've got all our best generals in the newspaper offices!" That's not a slam on newspaper people; but it is a good reminder that anyone who does anything significant is likely to be criticized by someone sitting on the sideline.

If you are "in the fields," even the fields of ministry, criticism will come. Our effectiveness in following our call will depend largely on how we respond to that criticism.

Many of us react angrily to criticism, dismissing it as irrelevant. Others of us are devastated by criticism, assuming that we deserve every last barb. Usually, the truth is somewhere between these two extremes. Most criticisms are worthy of neither arrogant dismissal nor uncritical acceptance.

Criticism isn't all bad. Criticism can be a good thing. It can be like those kiddie bumpers in the lanes at the bowling alley. Criticism, at least good criticism, keeps us headed toward the goal without falling into the gutter. It certainly is easier to be humble when we are being criticized. Criticism also initiates the kind of intense self-examination that call following requires. Moreover, criticism forces us to ask what *God* thinks of us. Therefore, criticism is not all bad.

How we receive criticism is also a pretty good barometer of our spiritual maturity. Either a knee-jerk reaction to condemnation, or a naive agreement with it, can signal that some character work needs to be done. Our response is particularly telling when the criticism is valid. When legitimate criticism stings, yet we turn around and try to meet the need expressed in that criticism, our moral fiber is strengthened and our effectiveness is wonderfully enhanced.

Don't let critics rob you of your call. As a missionary in Nigeria I learned a popular saying in the Yoruba language that in English is translated, "It pours cold water on my heart." We have to be careful not to let critics pour cold water on our hearts *when we are certain* that our hearts are right. Reggie McNeal wrote in *A Work of Heart,* "Some famous advice to Christian leaders through the years goes something like this: 'Behind every criticism, there lies a nugget of truth.' That is bad advice." McNeal is right; some criticism carries no truth, is not appropriate, and should be treated as such. Criticism can be completely unfounded. Don't let bad criticism dampen your sense of call.

Ask, "What's behind this criticism?" The motive behind the criticism makes a big difference in how we should respond. The following came from that model call follower Martin Luther King Jr. in his "Letter from Birmingham Jail," dated April 16, 1963, and was addressed to white clergy in the Birmingham area:

> If I sought to answer all of the criticisms that cross my desk, my secretaries would be engaged in little else during the course of the day, and I would have no time for constructive work....But since I feel that you are men of genuine goodwill and your criticisms are sincerely set forth, I would like to answer your statement in what I hope will be patient and reasonable terms.

Notice that the motives of these ministers, or at least what Dr. King perceived to be their motives, made a difference as to whether or not he responded. The way we respond to criticism ought to be determined largely by the motives of the critic.

Of course truth is truth, no matter who speaks it. Sometimes valid criticism comes from the mouths of hateful people. I'm not suggesting that we ignore criticism merely because we don't like someone's attitude.

Nevertheless, we must do our best to discern the motive of the critic. **If the one criticizing us has good motives—has our good at heart—then that person's criticism deserves a more careful hearing than the criticism of one who has impure intentions.**

Look for a pattern. One of the infamous critics in the Bible is Sanballat. Note his pattern:

- *"Sanballat...ridiculed us"* (Nehemiah 2:19).
- *"Sanballat...ridiculed the Jews"* (Nehemiah 4:1).
- *"Sanballat...plotted...to stir up trouble against [Jerusalem]"* (Nehemiah 4:7–8).
- *"Sanballat and Geshem...were scheming to harm me"* (Nehemiah 6:2).

Nehemiah, often the target of Sanballat's antagonism, paid no attention to Sanballat because, among other things, Sanballat was a habitual critic.

Some people are just negative by nature, and they have established a pattern. Yogi Berra, in his book *When You Come to a Fork in the Road, Take It!* speaks about how he dealt with umpires, both as a player then as a coach. He made the point that he had to choose when to harangue an umpire and when to keep his cool, because "people who disagree or argue all the time...lose credibility." Yogi nailed it. When a person is often complaining about something, that person forfeits his or her credibility. It's a bit like the boy who cried wolf; people who habitually criticize should be seen as contrary spirits. We shouldn't dismiss them outright, but we should think long and hard before we let a habitual critic change us, or wound us.

Over the years, I've been on the receiving end of my share of criticism (more than a little of it was well-deserved). There are people who, when they have come into my office with a criticism, have gotten my full attention, for they aren't critical by nature. There have been a few, however, who, over time, forfeited their right to a careful hearing because they exhibited a pattern of criticism.

Live so that unfair attacks on your character will be largely ignored. A person's life should speak for itself. This is affirmed by 1 Peter 3:16, *"Keeping a clear conscience so that those who speak maliciously against your behavior in Christ may be ashamed of their slander."*

President Abraham Lincoln once was falsely charged with a cold act of insensitivity. One of the President's friends, Ward Lamon, knew the truth and was furious. He encouraged the President to issue a public denial of the charges. Lincoln responded, "If I have not established a character enough to give the lie to this charge, I can only say that I am mistaken in my own estimate of myself." Our best defense against unfounded criticism is how we live every day.

Don't be overcome by criticism. Ben Patterson wrote, "If I can't remember the last time I was criticized for doing something, chances are I'm not doing anything significant. If my goal is simply to keep all the cattle mooing softly in the corral, I'm failing as a leader. But if you are moving them out on the trail toward Dodge City and points beyond, you can expect an occasional stampede or two."

If you attempt anything significant, you will be criticized. While there is no virtue in relishing opposition, the attempt to be admired can cost us our integrity. Jesus Himself warned: "Woe unto you when all men speak well of you." Criticism, therefore, should be accepted as a cost of call following.

Effective call followers are confident enough not to go on the defensive when confronted, and humble enough to know that some of the criticism is deserved. Yet they do not allow character assassins to rob them of their joy or distract them from their call. **Spiritual maturity allows us to take our medicine when we need to, yet not to swallow every bitter pill that comes our way.**

The effective call follower develops a tender heart, a tough hide, a clear mind, and a discerning ear. If you are without any one of the four, you are like a car running with one flat tire. I know of no way to develop that crucial combination of characteristics other than having (1) a close relationship with God; and (2) someone, or a small group of fellow call followers, who can assist us in our self-awareness.

CONFLICT WILL ERUPT

Conflict is inevitable any time humans spend time together. It is particularly likely when the stakes are high. Every story of compass-following adventurers I can remember includes elements of big-time conflict.

Conflict is more painful in a Christian organization, however. We just don't expect Christ followers to bicker and battle. Squabbles at the office? Sure. On the wilderness trail? Certainly. But at church?

Larry McSwain and William Treadwell wrote a book with the title, *Conflict Ministry in the Church.* In that book they wrote that conflict occurs most often in congregations in which there is a deep commitment to the church. When there is apathy, there is no conflict. Corpses, the authors said, don't fight!

Conflict in the church is not the end of the world. Nor should conflict be surprising. Nevertheless, for most of us, conflict is agony. In fact, the Greek word for conflict is *agon*, from which the English word *agony* comes. Heated confrontations, heated discussions, heated relationships, always are agonizing. They are just *more* agonizing when they occur in Christian circles.

Studies have shown that those of us drawn to vocational ministry have personalities that loathe conflict. I have a hunch that is true of many who follow a call to volunteer ministry as well. Therefore, fulfilling our call requires a mature perspective on conflict and an intentional willingness to face it. We can survive, and even grow from, the inevitable difficulties in relationships with the following of a few basic principles.

Maintain grace under pressure. Ernest Hemingway defined courage as "grace under pressure." That kind of response is exactly what is needed from call followers when conflict erupts.

A friend of mine years ago was asked to leave his position. By the time he spoke with me, it didn't matter who was at fault. That he needed to leave was clear, and he'd been given time to find another place of ministry.

So when he honored me by asking for advice I responded, "Leave with grace. Between now and the time you leave, people will be watching you. You have the potential to have a greater influence in people's lives now than ever before. People will pay attention to how you act under duress. They will watch to see if you act out of resentment, striking back at those who have attacked you, or if you maintain your dignity, and leave with grace." I was proud of him and his remaining time there, for he did conduct himself with dignity. He was gracious and a Christian gentleman. Perhaps he will be remembered more for the way he conducted himself in those few months leading up to his departure than in all his years prior to that.

Call followers come under careful scrutiny when we are involved in a conflict. I hope observers can say we have maintained grace under pressure.

Own your part of the conflict. A strong sense of call, and confidence in our identity, are essential. Those very strengths, however, can be liabilities. They can blind us to our own contributions to conflicts. **There is a fine line, for example, between an unflappable commitment to our call and a stubborn refusal to consider opposing viewpoints.**

Therefore, the first question the call follower must ask is, "What is it about *me* that is causing this problem? Have I been too pushy? Have I been unwilling to hear people out? Does my personality have a bit of an edge?"

This self-examination prevents our jumping to the conclusion that the fault for conflict rests with someone else. Then, if we are at least partially responsible for the conflict, we can adjust our attitudes. (I can't change someone else, but I can let God change *me*.) Moreover, acknowledgment of our contributions to the strife often neutralizes other parties' hostility.

I really like the book, *Don't Let Jerks Get the Best of You.* I bought it thinking it would help me deal with difficult people. I was enjoying the book until, a mere 24 pages into it, I got to the "Self-Jerk-Test." Imagine my surprise to find that I have some fairly jerky tendencies myself! It's not easy, for it goes against my nature, but I have to own my part of any conflict.

Know that being a doormat is not a virtue. Jesus told us to be "innocent as doves," but in that same sentence He cautioned us to be "shrewd as serpents" (Matthew 10:16). Being a doormat, you see, is not a Christian virtue. The willingness to let people treat us like doormats often grows out of a feeling that we are not worthy of better. That is why some women remain in horribly abusive relationships—and why others of us put up with abuse of a less dramatic nature—because we feel we don't deserve more.

Paul Meier, a well-known Christian physician, wrote the book mentioned above, *Don't Let Jerks Get the Best of You.* The book certainly does not encourage us to violate the Bible's guidelines on love and humility. Yet the book does say that God never intended you to allow jerky people to abuse you. The Bible says that followers of Jesus are supposed to be meek and gentle. That doesn't mean we are to be wimps, or unduly subservient.

Humility is a Christian virtue. Being a doormat is not.

Practice gentleness. What is it that thrills us about seeing lions perform in the circus? It is their gentleness! These powerful beasts are jumping around like poodles, and "taking it" when the tamer cracks his whip. Why does that so electrify us? It is their gentleness—the fact that they could attack the tamer, but they don't. Why do we hold our breaths when the trainer sticks his head between the mighty jaws of the king of the jungle? It is the lion's gentleness! There, before our eyes, is an animal that has meat-eating instincts and the power to have lion-tamer croquettes for dinner. But the beast is choosing not to exercise its power.

Gentleness in the New Testament is the intentional bridling or harnessing of strength. The Greek word that is translated "gentleness" in the Bible is the word *prautes*. *Prautes*, among other things, means "tame," and in New Testament days was used of animals—powerful animals that, by nature, were aggressive, but that had been tamed, or gentled.

Gentleness, then, according to its New Testament origins, is the intentional bridling or harnessing of our strength in order to defer to the needs of another. Gentleness is the strength of restraint. James 3:17 (NRSV) reads, *"But the wisdom from above is first pure, then peaceable, gentle, willing to yield, full of mercy and good fruits."* Gentleness means yielding to another, when we don't have to, for the cause of the greater good.

There is a dangerous spot near the entrance to the neighborhood where I live. Those coming off the main road have the right of way. Drivers on the cross street have the yield sign. But not many people driving on that cross street choose to yield; they come right through. It's as if people in the neighborhood got together and declared the yield sign on that cross street "invalid."

So if you ever come to see us, be careful at that intersection. Yield even when you don't have to; it would be easy to get killed there with the right of way. Of course you have every right to keep going even if another car is plowing through. If it makes you feel better, should you meet your Maker at that precarious corner, we'll put this on your tombstone: "Here lies one who had the right of way!"

Gentleness is coming up to an intersection of sorts in a discussion or a relationship, and knowing you are right. You would be completely justified if you were to impose your will or insist on the last word. You have both the right and the power to put that scalawag in his or her place. But to do so would absolutely wreck the relationship, devastate the person, and/or harm the cause of God's kingdom. Gentleness says, "I know I have the right of way here, but this issue is not worth the conflict, so I am going to yield to the other person for his or her good and the good of the cause."

In Matthew 11:29, Jesus said, *"Learn from me, for I am gentle and humble in heart."* Jesus is the model of gentleness. Instead of breaking into history riding a meteor accompanied by angelic trumpets, Jesus eased gently into our world through a teenager's womb and an innkeeper's stall. **Instead of demanding the treatment He rightfully deserved, He walked where He went and slept where He could and ate what was offered and taught who would listen.**

Then the greatest demonstration of His gentleness came on the night prior to, and the day of, His crucifixion.

"To this you were called, because Christ suffered for you, leaving you an example, that you should follow in his steps.... When they hurled their insults at him, he did not retaliate;

when he suffered, he made no threats. Instead, he entrusted himself to him who judges justly" (1 Peter 2:21, 23).

Jesus was gentle, and it was not for lack of power. He didn't strike back when the soldiers beat him. He didn't yell back when the crowds heckled him. He kept His cool even with the saliva of Roman soldiers running down His face. He endured the pain and humiliation of an old, rugged cross when, as the old gospel song says, "He could have called ten-thousand angels" to rescue Him.

Jesus was *gentle,* in the true sense of the word. He was gentle even when He was criticized and even when He was in conflict.

Recognize whether this is an organizational issue or a personal issue. If the conflict is a personal issue, then the gentle response generally would be to yield. However, if the conflict threatens the health and mission of the organization, then you cannot afford to overlook it.

Let's consider a fictitious incident with "Joanna" as an example. Joanna is chairperson of her church's Missions Committee. Joab, one of the church curmudgeons, is a member of that group.

One night, in the Missions Committee meeting, Joanna suggests that the church organize a churchwide mission trip to her home state of Wyoming. The church has been talking about just such a project, and she knows how much help her home area could use. Her suggestion gets a fairly warm response...except from Joab. Joab declares it is too far to go and the trip is too expensive.

Joab, this burr under Joanna's saddle, is at it again. He

has torpedoed her suggestions before. Joanna thinks first of strangling him, but reconsiders when she figures there are too many witnesses present. Furthermore, Joab does have a point about the expense and distance; Joanna had thought about that herself.

Doggone it, Joanna thinks, Joab is going to get his way again. She knows that the other members of the committee will vote for the Wyoming trip if she pushes the issue. She is, after all, a popular influencer in the congregation. Yet this is neither the place nor time for a showdown. And this is more of a personal thing between Joab and Joanna. So she decides to yield; she withdraws her suggestion about a mission trip to Wyoming.

In the next monthly meeting, Jeanette, another member of the Missions Committee, addresses the church's vision for planting a new congregation. For two years the Missions Committee has been pondering, praying, and preparing for the launching of a new church. Everything is coming together, and consensus is growing that the time is right to move ahead with the launch. Jeanette makes a formal motion that their church plan for the first worship service of the new congregation six months from that date.

Joab speaks. He doesn't like the idea. "There's plenty to do around here," he whines. "And we can't fill all our committees now! What if some of our best givers go out to start a new church? They'll take their wallets with them, you know!"

A cold wind blows into the room. The church has had this vision of a new church for a long time. But, gosh, no one wants a fight.

Joanna again considers her response. This time it's not personal between herself and Joab. There is more at stake than Joanna's pride; this time the values of the church are in jeopardy. Eternal destinies literally hang in the balance. The mission and vision of the church are in question.

Joab has been known to speak in such unpleasant tones that people are intimidated. Some have quietly referred to his behavior as bullying, but never to his face. Few have the desire, and nobody has had the nerve, to confront Joab with his behavior. A few years ago there was a painful church split, and everyone is afraid it will happen again. Every time Joab raises his voice, people cringe at the very possibility of another fight. Joab has had his way over the last couple of years, and the church is suffering for it. A few families have left, frustrated that leaders have allowed Joab and a few others like him to hijack the church. The previous pastor was relieved when he received an invitation to become pastor of another church, and the present pastor is dispirited. No one, however, has done anything about Joab.

Joanna sits in the committee meeting remembering those days when she was praying about the invitation to lead this Missions Committee. Her sense of call was so clear she told her husband, "I feel like my call is as certain as that which our missionaries experience." When she said yes, it was with an unequivocal sense of divine leadership. Now, her call and the congregation's call overlap. She cannot ignore the church's call without somewhat abandoning her own.

The matter of the new church is tabled, and Joanna decides to act before the next meeting. She asks to meet with Joab at the church, and tells him that she will be bringing the minister of missions with her. As the meeting begins Joanna acknowledges that her attitude toward Joab has not always been conciliatory. "I admit that it has been hard for me to be objective in my disagreements with you. I'm sure that my attitude and approach have not always been appropriate. For that I apologize. The matter I'd like to discuss today, however, has to do with the church's mission, not our personal differences."

Joanna continues gently, but there is an unmistakable resolve in her voice. "Joab," she says, "I don't doubt your passion for our church. But your intimidating ways have hurt us. We have gotten sidetracked and even lost some good people because of your menacing style.

"Now," she continues after a big breath, "the overwhelming majority of our church members believe God is calling us to plant a new congregation, and I believe that is indeed what God wants us to do. As chairperson of the Missions Committee, it is my responsibility to help the church fulfill our calling and I intend to carry out my responsibility. In our next meeting we are going to vote on that new church, and I expect that the vote will be in the affirmative. I hope that you, as a faithful member of that committee, will abide by the committee's decision even if you disagree. I also hope you will get on board with this ministry, for you have a lot to offer our church."

Joanna came prepared to tell Joab that, should he try to sabotage the committee's action, she would ask the church leaders to handle the matter. She had been studying texts like Titus 3:10 which instruct the church not to allow troublemakers to cause discord in the congregation. Joanna decided, however, not to be so confrontational quite yet.

When asked if he wanted to respond, Joab declined. After a rather strained leave taking, Joanna walked out of the room with her palms sweating and her heart racing. She had looked a bully in the eye and spoken plain truth in a gracious way.

Six weeks later the church, upon the recommendation of the Missions Committee, enthusiastically agreed to plant the new congregation. Joab left the church. The church has regained its sense of mission and even welcomed back some of those who had left. The last they heard of Joab, he was causing trouble in another place.

One of the interesting truths about call following is that people can look at the same compass, agree on the direction, and still disagree passionately over how the journey should be undertaken. A commitment to the call often requires skill in handling dissension.

There are times when we have to let people be people. All of us are going to lose our patience and say something out of line from time to time. There is a time to yield, to restrain from having our way just because we can.

Nevertheless, when someone is being destructive—for instance, when the church is suffering because of someone's bullying—then it is time to exercise tough love. Then it is time to say, graciously, "We cannot let you get away with that." Jesus prayed that we would be one, but we cannot focus on that oneness to the extent that peace becomes an obsession, or even the ultimate goal. **Tranquillity does not trump the Great Commission.**

The beautiful, Old Testament concept of *shalom* is not the mere absence of conflict. It is the presence of justice and integrity—the existence of honest relationships, community, and wholeness. If an organization's mission is sacrificed for the sake of a troublemaker or two, then that is not *shalom*. That, in the words of Ken Sande, is not peace*making*; it is peace*faking*.

GOOD LIVING AND GOOD DYING

13

One day, one breath will be our last.
Remembering that is not a bad thing.
"Teach us to number our days aright,"
wrote the psalmist, "that we may gain
a heart of wisdom" (Psalm 90:12).

There is a legend of a king named Philip who had a slave to whom King Philip gave a standing order. The slave was to come to the king every morning, no matter the day, and no matter what the king was doing, and the slave was to announce, "Philip, remember that thou must die!" That was the slave's daily task.

King Philip wanted to be reminded every morning that we would die one day, so that he would live accordingly.

That little slave is still running around. Maybe you have seen him, or at least heard him whisper. During the night he sneaks into the rooms of people my age and paints our hairs white, one by one. Sometimes he gently pulls them out and leaves them on our pillows. And when we awake to our hair crisis the little slave whispers from the shadows, "Remember, you must die."

A woman notices that the wrinkles are becoming increasingly prominent, so she reaches again for her age-defying cream and applies it liberally before lying down. As she lies there that little slave whispers from the dark corner, "Remember, you must die."

A middle-aged man loses a friend to a heart attack and lies in his bed that night trying to go to sleep. The little slave crawls up under the covers with him and whispers in his ear, "Remember, you must die."

He seldom speaks to young people, but even they sometimes see one of their schoolmates fall to a heartless disease or die in an automobile accident. They go to school and look over at the empty desk where their friend used to sit. Then they look again and, sitting in that desk is that little slave. He looks over and whispers, "Remember that you, too, must die."

That little slave is not very popular with us. But here is the good part: that little slave is not the enemy. Why did King Philip want that little slave to remind him of the certainty and imminence of his death? Because he wanted to live with the reminder that he didn't have forever on the earth. That's not a bad thing to be reminded of every morning. Charles E. Poole understood that, and wrote in *Don't Cry Past Tuesday:* "To live each day as though someday life is going to end is to live with a healthy sense of urgency and an appropriate sense of insecurity that makes us treat life for what it is: a precious, passing, limited gift from God."

John Keating, an innovative teacher played by Robin Williams in the movie *Dead Poets Society*, helped his students to understand that. The teacher gathered his students in the hallway of the school, telling them to look closely at the pictures of the alumni in the trophy case, many of whom were strapping athletes in those fading photos. Those young, invincible guys now were "fertilizing daffodils," Keating said. The teacher asked his students what they wanted to do with their lives in the light of the fact that they aren't going to live forever. Then he uttered those well-known words from the movie, "*Carpe diem!* Seize the day. Make your lives extraordinary." He taught his students to "seize the day" in light of the fact that their day would not last forever.

What would you do if you were to realize, I mean really realize, that you aren't going to be here forever? How would you "seize the day"? Would you need to change your lifestyle to focus on what is important?

Have you heard Tim McGraw's song, "Live Like You Were Dying"? It is a country music song about a man who, in his early 40s, had a frightening medical diagnosis and realized how preciously short life is. One of the lines in the song says, "Someday I hope you get the chance to live like you were dying."

Country music sometimes has some pretty good theology.

I have a fairly large, framed photograph of my father when he was about my age or a little younger. It is a shot of my dad and the men on his shift at his workplace. He looks wonderfully strong and full of life. In the photo, his hair is not nearly as gray as my hair is now.

But he became an old man. And he died. One day I will die too. That photograph reminds me to live like I am dying —to cram all the call I can into this life, which I seem to be living in fast-forward.

You have a call from the Creator of the universe. He has gifted you and placed a fire of some sort in your belly. Your abilities intersect with some of the world's needs and God has blessed you with the privilege of a place in His mission. **You have a divine call. What you do *not* have is unlimited time to fulfill that call.**

Have you heard that little slave whisper lately?

THE JOY OF MEANINGFUL SERVICE

Paul wrote, in Ephesians 5:15–16, *"Be very careful, then, how you live—not as unwise but as wise, making the most of every opportunity."* You and I miss out on a lot of opportunities by spending time—often a lot of time—on things that aren't that important.

Television screens and computer screens, the iPod and the brick façade, what the neighbors think and what the neighbors drive, paychecks and paybacks—they all can distract us from what is important in life. Our calling in life—what God created us to be and do—*that* is important. A meaningful life is an intentional, missional life. And one of the great benefits of intentional, missional living is joy!

C. S. Lewis, in *Surprised by Joy,* suggested that joy is not found when it is sought, so much as it is a "byproduct whose very existence presupposes that you desire not it but something other and outer." **Joy is the almost unexpected consequence of meaningful pursuits.** Joy is found in giving ourselves for purposes that are greater than ourselves and that have everlasting consequences. Getting so lost in an eternal cause that we forget to complain about how the world is not making us happy—that's joy.

Jesus is our example here. Hebrews 12:2 says, *"Let us fix our eyes on Jesus, the author and perfecter of our faith, who for the joy set before him endured the cross, scorning its shame, and sat down at the right hand of the throne of God."* I believe this is talking about more than His joyful assurance of a resurrection. I believe Jesus found joy in giving His life. Was it fun? Obviously not; but don't mistake fun for joy. Jesus, under the pressure and physical pain and emotional hell of taking upon Himself our sin, still found a deep joy, for He loves us and knew what His sacrificial death would mean for us.

Joy at its deepest comes with the willingness to give our lives for that which C. S. Lewis called "other and outer"— a cause that is beyond ourselves—a call that requires a costly investment, yet pays its dividends in joy.

FINISHING THE COURSE WITH JOY

"I have fought the good fight, I have finished the race, I have kept the faith" (2 Timothy 4:7).

"But none of these things move me, neither count I my life dear unto myself, so that I might finish my course with joy, and the ministry, which I have received of the Lord Jesus, to testify the gospel of the grace of God" (Acts 20:24 KJV).

Can you imagine what it was like when Lewis and Clark reached the Pacific in 1805? After following their compass through the wilderness, across the rivers, the Rockies, and the rough country, they reached the end of their journey. Clark wrote, on November 7, "Great joy in camp we are in View of Ocian [sic]." That joy at the end of the course surely was worth all the hardships they had endured along the way.

If we are following our God-given calls, then there will be a great sense of fulfillment at the end of our own journeys as well. **Would it not be deeply satisfying to come to the end of the line on earth and look back with a sense that we had done all we were called to do, when and where we were called to do it?** On the other hand, how sad it would be to come to the end of our journey and hear God whisper, *"While you were doing all these things...I spoke to you again and again, but you did not listen; I called you, but you did not answer"* (Jeremiah 7:13).

Not long ago I had an MRI; they wanted to look at my head. It was painless, but awfully noisy. (The MRI showed no signs of any problem; the doctors were just being especially cautious, for which I am especially grateful.)

I spent a good long while lying still on my back with rather intimidating sounds going on around me, and I had this thought: What if they find something that doesn't look right? What if the technician behind that glass comes into this room with a "bless your heart" look on his face? What if the neurologist reads the results of this MRI and has bad news for me?

I thought...and I think I was being honest...I'm not afraid to die. I'd be terribly sad, sure. I'd be bummed out. I'd go through all the stages of grief. I'd deny it. I'd be mad about it. And I'd fight for my life. But I am not afraid to die.

Don't get me wrong. My confidence comes not because I think I'm such a good guy. As I confessed earlier, I get my priorities out of order and I act selfishly and sometimes my motives are not pure. I'm a child of God who makes sinful choices more often than I'd like to admit. And

I do wish I'd made some different decisions, particularly during my high school and college days. But here's the deal: I have followed God's call. I feel like I've lived a much fuller life than a lot of people who are far older than I, simply because I have followed God's call. I've not followed it perfectly, and I should have done some things differently. Nevertheless, call following has removed the sting of death.

THE ANTICIPATION OF ETERNAL REWARDS

We don't like to think about death. Some of us are on our personal death-prevention programs. We go to the gym and we jog. We take vitamins and eat bran muffins. We buy wrinkle smoother-outers and age spot cover-uppers. We'll do just about anything if we think we can postpone, or at least forget, our appointment with death.

We dress up death. We disguise death with flowers and new suits and expensive caskets and airtight vaults. Some just have a hard time thinking about death. Some of us, in fact, are downright scared of death. Rarely do we talk about it.

We don't even talk much about heaven, do we? Except at funerals maybe, or when we hear of someone's death. You'll hear plenty of jokes about St. Peter and the pearly gates, but very few genuine conversations about heaven. Maybe it's because we fear talk of heaven might make us appear weak, or corny, or unlearned. For whatever reason, you don't hear a lot about heaven. Even within the Christian family, we don't talk much about heaven.

That's a shame, for the old gospel song is right regarding followers of Jesus: *"This world is not our home; we're just a-passin' through."* If we aren't careful, we will begin to think we belong here.

When we moved to Nigeria, our son Grant was ten months old. When he was four we were preparing to return to the United States (US) for our first vacation. He heard all the talk about packing and preparing to go to the US, and he asked me one day, "Daddy, have you ever been to the United States?" Grant was so "Nigerian," and we had talked about the place of our citizenship so little, I guess, Grant got the idea that Nigeria was home.

If we don't remind ourselves from time to time where our citizenship lies, we might think this earth is home! That would be a shame, for the greatest rewards for call following do not come in this life. The ultimate rewards come, for the one whose faith is in Jesus, just beyond our last breath of this earth's air. Of course I don't know exactly how the rewards thing is going to work out.

I got the chance to spend two weeks in Europe on a choir trip during the summer after my graduation from high school. When we visited some of the museums and historic places, those who had put the time and sacrifice into being good students were awed by what they saw. They were seeing what they had so diligently studied in their classes. Gazing upon the great structures and masterpieces of the Old World was a remarkably rewarding experience for them.

I'm ashamed to say that I had not been a good student to that point. And I can't say that I was all that impressed with all the art and old buildings. I was more interested in the sopranos and altos than in the statues and architecture. Those good students and I were standing in the same places, enjoying the same experiences—yet they had a greater capacity than I had for enjoying those experiences.

Perhaps that is what it will be like in heaven—all of us enjoying the same experiences, but some having a greater capacity for rewards than others. My hunch is that those who are faithfully following their calls are building up the aptitude for far more rewarding experiences than others will enjoy.

We cannot be sure of the way rewards will be doled out in heaven, but the Bible is clear that rewards await those whose faith is in Jesus. One of the most intriguing thoughts about what rewards await us comes from a story I found in my research on the history of missionary work in Nigeria.

In the 1860s, there was a terrible war between two tribes in the land we now call Nigeria. Andrew Phillips was a missionary who helped minister to the people of the town of Ijaiye who were injured, orphaned, or displaced by the war.

One day he was summoned to the home of a dying man—a man he had led to faith in Jesus. Realizing that death was near, the man said to the missionary, "Soon I will die. But I will go to heaven. When I reach the gates the angels will carry me to the Lord Jesus. When I thank Jesus for His mercy, I will come back to the gate and wait for you. When you come, I will not allow the angels to carry you. **These arms will carry you to the Lord Jesus, and I will tell Him, 'This is the missionary that preached the gospel to this poor sinner.'"**

I don't mean to be melodramatic or theatrical or unduly sentimental. (And I can't vouch for the theological soundness of the Nigerian man's promise.) However, I thought it might help for you to be reminded that there will come a day when you will be wonderfully rewarded for your faithfulness to God's call.

There are a lot of wonderful benefits to remembering that heaven awaits.

Remembering that heaven awaits reminds us why the longings of our souls are not completely satisfied in this world.

There are desires within us that no experience in this world can satisfy. So if you long for such things as love that is pure, peace that is perfect, and joy that is boundless, then you will have to be patient. You were made for another world, and you're not home yet.

Sometimes in the food court at the mall or in the deli section at the grocery store someone will be standing there with samples on toothpicks. You know that little cube of cheese or smoked sausage cannot satisfy your hunger. It is but a taste of something available beyond that point that is delicious and satisfying. In the same way, even the best of experiences here are only, in the words of the hymn, "a foretaste of glory divine." Fanny Crosby wrote, "There are depths of love that I cannot know till I cross the narrow sea; there are heights of joy that I may not reach till I rest in peace with Thee."

Remembering that heaven awaits helps us keep our priorities straight.

Some have said, "We don't want to be so heavenly minded that we are of no earthly good," and I understand that sentiment; but if we are totally focused on this world, then we will spend too much time on things that aren't really important. Wayne Cordeiro wrote in *Doing Church as a Team*:

> To contrast the brevity of our earthly existence with that of eternity, I would take out my ballpoint pen and draw a vertical scratch on the extended cable. Then I would tell you that the width of that scratch mark (about $1/32$ of an inch) represents the length of our life on Earth compared with eternity. Not very long!
>
> But do you know what most people do? They not only live on that scratch, but they also love that scratch....They live scratch lives, have scratch businesses, raise scratch families with scratch hopes and scratch dreams....
>
> ...They try to elongate it, stretch it and extend it as much as possible. But even in the midst of their attempts, they know deep inside that there's got to be something more.

Living for that "scratch" gets our priorities all inverted. Remembering that this world is a mere blip on the radar screen of eternity helps us keep the main thing *the main thing*.

Remembering that heaven awaits gives us courage.

"Do not let not your hearts be troubled," Jesus said in John 14:1. And in 2 Corinthians 5:6, 8 we read, *"We are always confident and know that as long as we are at home in the body we are away from the Lord....We are confident, I say, and would prefer to be away from the body and at home with the Lord."* "Confident," here, is a translation of the Greek word *thareo*, which can mean "confident," as it is translated in the New International Version. More specifically, it means "taking courage."

John Bunyan wrote *The Pilgrim's Progress* as an allegory of the journey, or pilgrimage, of Christ followers. It is the story of Christian, a man on a journey toward the Celestial City. On his journey he suffered from all kinds of problems. He fell into the Valley of Humiliation, sank into the Swamp of Despondency, and got locked up in Doubting Castle. When someone asked how he overcame his feelings of discouragement, Christian answered, "When my thoughts turn to where I am going, that will do it." That which encouraged Christian through the hard times was the assurance of where he was going—that he was on his way to heaven, the Celestial City. Followers of Jesus can take courage, even when we're in the valley, the swamp, or the castle, by remembering where we're going.

Remembering that heaven awaits encourages us to hold on.

"I press on toward the goal to win the prize for which God has called me heavenward in Christ Jesus" (Philippians 3:14). During a shameful chapter of our nation's history, people who had been shipped from Africa struggled to survive physically, emotionally, and spiritually. And from those victims of unbridled greed have come inspiring stories of faith.

Slaves overheard the sermons and stories of eternal salvation at the churches and camp meetings of their owners. Somehow they were able to see beyond their owners' hypocrisy to the truth of the message. That message of salvation touched chords deep in the slaves' hearts, and the promise of rewards in a world beyond this one were particularly heartening. Truths about a land called heaven gave them hope. One of my favorite spirituals has to do with that hope, and is based on Jesus's words in Luke 9. I wish I had a recording of slaves singing:

> *I never been to heaven but I been told*
> *The streets up there are lined with gold.*
> *Keep your hand on that plow, hold on.*

It sounds old-fashioned I know, but I would encourage you to remember your reward in heaven, and be faithful to your call. *Keep your hand on that plow and hold on.*

My mother grew up in Alabama, on Sand Mountain, on a farm. When Mom was in elementary school, the school organized a trip for the students to go to the state Capitol in Montgomery. It's hard for most of us to know what a big deal that was for a poor little country girl from Blount County, Alabama, in the late 1920s. That would be like one of us getting a personal invitation to the White House.

The day of the trip came and, for some reason, Mom was a few minutes late in arriving at the school. My guess is she had to finish her farm chores and just didn't get there on time.

When it was almost time to leave, the teacher stood at the front of the bus with the class roll. The teacher began to read the names. (Mom wouldn't find out until later what happened.)

The teacher began to read. As she read, eager students answered. "Johnny Able?" "Here." "Suzy Blackwood?" "Here."

"Maude Copeland?" (That was my mom's name.)

When the teacher called "Maude Copeland" some impatient little girl in the back of the bus answered, "Here."

The teacher didn't look up and, assuming that little Maude Copeland was on the bus, continued down the list. When there had been a "here" for every name, they closed the door and the bus left for Montgomery. Maude arrived at the school a few minutes later to be told that the bus had left. There would be no trip for her that day. She turned around and walked the long walk home.

Can you imagine what it must have been like for a little country girl, probably carrying her bag of biscuits for lunch, to show up at the school and find that the bus already had pulled out? Can you imagine her broken heart as she made the long, lonely trek back to the farmhouse?

Then, almost eight decades later, on a Thursday afternoon in August of 2004, when the Creator of the universe called her name, it was *she* who answered, "Here."

When I was little I'd hear her sing:

> *When the trumpet of the Lord shall sound, and time*
> *shall be no more,*
> *And the morning breaks eternal, bright, and fair;*
> *When the saved of earth shall gather over on the other*
> *shore,*
> *And the roll is called up yonder I'll be there.*

One afternoon it was...and she was.

One day the roll will be called for you too. So run the remainder of your course with the assurance of a joy that exceeds our imaginations...just beyond that *final call*.

New Hope® Publishers is a division of WMU®, an international organization that challenges Christian believers to understand and be radically involved in God's mission. For more information about WMU, go to www.wmu.com. More information about New Hope books may be found at www.newhopepublishers.com. New Hope books may be purchased at your local bookstore.